# Psychoanalysis and Psychoanalytic Therapies

## Second Edition

# Theories of Psychotherapy Series

**Theories of Psychotherapy Series**

Matt Englar-Carlson, Series Editor

# Psychoanalysis and Psychoanalytic Therapies

## Second Edition

Jeremy D. Safran and
Jennifer Hunter

 **AMERICAN PSYCHOLOGICAL ASSOCIATION**

Published by
American Psychological Association
750 First Street, NE
Washington, DC 20002
https://www.apa.org

Order Department
https://www.apa.org/pubs/books
order@apa.org

In the U.K., Europe, Africa, and the Middle East, copies may be ordered from Eurospan
https://www.eurospanbookstore.com/apa
info@eurospangroup.com

Typeset in Minion by Circle Graphics, Inc., Reisterstown, MD

Printer: Sheridan Books, Chelsea, MI
Cover Designer: Beth Schlenoff, Bethesda, MD

**Library of Congress Cataloging-in-Publication Data**
Names: Safran, Jeremy D., author. | Hunter, Jennifer (Psychologist), author.
Title: Psychoanalysis and psychoanalytic therapies / Jeremy D. Safran and
  Jennifer Hunter.
Description: Second Edition. | Washington : American Psychological
  Association, 2020. | Series: Theories of psychotherapy series | Revised edition
  of Psychoanalysis and psychoanalytic therapies, c2012. | Includes bibliographical
  references and index.
Identifiers: LCCN 2020001139 (print) | LCCN 2020001140 (ebook) |
  ISBN 9781433832321 (paperback) | ISBN 9781433832345 (ebook)
Subjects: LCSH: Psychoanalysis. | Psychotherapy.
Classification: LCC BF173 .S257 2020 (print) | LCC BF173 (ebook) |
  DDC 150.19/5—dc23
LC record available at https://lccn.loc.gov/2020001139
LC ebook record available at https://lccn.loc.gov/2020001140

http://dx.doi.org/10.1037/0000190-000

*Printed in the United States of America*

10 9 8 7 6 5 4 3 2 1

For my daughters, Ayla and Ellie, who liked to tease me
about having "all those Freud books" lying around the house.

—*Jeremy D. Safran*

For Marvin Hunter, whose adventurous spirit, lively intellect,
and unconditional support formed and sustained me.

—*Jennifer Hunter*

# Contents

# Series Preface

## Matt Englar-Carlson

Some might argue that in the contemporary clinical practice of psychotherapy, the focus on evidence-based intervention and effective outcome has overshadowed theory in importance. Maybe. But at the same time, it is clear that psychotherapists adopt and practice according to one theory or another because their experience, and decades of empirical evidence, suggests that having a sound theory of psychotherapy leads to greater therapeutic success. Theory is fundamental in guiding psychotherapists in understanding *why* people behave, think, and feel in certain ways, and it provides the guidance to then contemplate *what* a client can do to instigate meaningful change. Still, the role of theory in the helping process itself can be hard to explain. This narrative about solving problems may help convey theory's importance:

> Aesop tells the fable of the sun and wind having a contest to decide who was the most powerful. From above the earth, they spotted a person walking down the street, and the wind said that he bet he could get his coat off. The sun agreed to the contest. The wind blew, and the person held on tightly to his coat. The more the wind blew, the tighter the person held on to his coat. The sun said it was his turn. He put all of his energy into creating warm sunshine, and soon the person took off his coat.

What does a competition between the sun and the wind to get the person to remove a coat have to do with theories of psychotherapy?

This deceptively simple story highlights the importance of theory as the precursor to any effective intervention—and hence to a favorable outcome. Without a guiding theory, a psychotherapist might treat the symptom without understanding the role of the individual. Or we might create power conflicts with our clients and not understand that, at times, indirect means of helping (sunshine) are often as effective as—if not more so than—direct ones (wind). In the absence of theory, a psychotherapist might lose track of the treatment rationale and instead get caught up in, for example, social correctness and not wanting to do something that looks too simple.

What exactly *is* theory? The *APA Dictionary of Psychology, Second Edition* defines theory as "a principle or body of interrelated principles that purports to explain or predict a number of interrelated phenomena" (VandenBos, 2015, p. 1081). In psychotherapy, a theory is a set of principles used to explain human thought and behavior, including what causes people to change. In practice, a theory frames the goals of therapy and specifies how to pursue them. Haley (1997) noted that a theory of psychotherapy ought to be simple enough for the average psychotherapist to understand but comprehensive enough to account for a wide range of eventualities. Furthermore, a theory guides action toward successful outcomes while generating hope in both the psychotherapist and client that recovery is possible.

Theory is the compass that allows psychotherapists to navigate the vast territory of clinical practice. In the same ways that navigational tools have been modified to adapt to advances in thinking and ever-expanding territories to explore, theories of psychotherapy have evolved over time to account for advances in science and technology. The different schools of theories are commonly referred to as *waves*—the first wave of psychodynamic theories (i.e., Adlerian, psychoanalytic), the second wave of learning theories (i.e., behavioral, cognitive-behavioral), the third wave of humanistic theories (i.e., person centered, gestalt, existential), the fourth wave of feminist and multicultural theories, and the fifth wave of postmodern and constructivist theories (i.e., narrative, constructivist). In many ways, these waves represent how psychotherapy has adapted and responded to changes in psychology, society, and epistemology, as well as to changes in the nature of psychotherapy itself. The wide variety of theories is also a testament to the different ways in which the same human behavior can be conceptualized depending on the view one espouses (Frew & Spiegler, 2012). Our theories of psychotherapy are also challenged to expand beyond the primarily Western worldview endemic in most psychotherapy theories and the practice of psychotherapy itself. That revision and correction requires theories and psychotherapists to become more inclusive of the full range of human diversity to reflect an understanding of human behavior that accounts for a client's context, identity, and intersectionality (American Psychological Association, 2017). To that end, psychotherapy and the theories that guide it are dynamic and responsive to the changing world around us.

With these two concepts in mind—the central importance of theory and the natural evolution of theoretical thinking—the APA Theories of Psychotherapy Series was developed. This series was created by my father (Jon Carlson) and me. Although educated in different eras, we both had a love of theory and often spent time discussing the range of complex ideas that drove each model. Even though my father identified strongly as an Adlerian and I was parented and raised from the Adlerian perspective, my father always espoused an appreciation for other theories and theorists—and that is something I picked up from him. As university faculty members teaching courses on the theories of psychotherapy, we wanted to create learning materials that not only highlighted the essence of the major theories for professionals and professionals in training but also clearly brought the reader up-to-date on the current status of the models, future directions with an emphasis on the inclusive application of the theories with clients representing the range of identities. Often in books on theory, the biography of the original theorist overshadows the evolution of the model. In contrast, our intent was to highlight the contemporary uses of the theories as well as their history and context—both past and present.

As this project began, we faced two immediate decisions: which theories to address and who best to present them. We assessed graduate-level theories of psychotherapy courses to see which theories are being taught, and we explored popular scholarly books, articles, and conferences to determine which theories draw the most interest. We then developed a dream list of authors from among the best minds in contemporary theoretical practice. To that end, each author in the series is one of the leading proponents of that approach as well as a knowledgeable practitioner. We asked each author to review the core constructs of the theory, bring the theory into the modern sphere of clinical practice by looking at it through a context of evidence-based practice, and clearly illustrate how the theory looks in application.

There are 24 titles planned for the series, and many titles are now in their second edition. Each title can stand alone or can be put together with a few other titles to create materials for a course in psychotherapy theories. This option allows instructors to create a course featuring the approaches they believe are the most salient today. To support this end, APA Books has also developed a video for each of the approaches to demonstrate the theory in practice with a real client. Many of the videos show psychotherapy over six sessions with the same client. Contact APA Books for a complete list of available video programs (https://www.apa.org/pubs/videos).

Preparing the preface for this second edition is quite bittersweet. Humanity lost a true leader and kind soul in the passing of Jeremy Safran. Jeremy and I had talked about crafting the second edition of this book in way that would draw more focus to social justice and the culturally responsive aspects of psychoanalytic practice. I was excited about this, but also a bit wary. Jeremy was not the easiest author to work with, but the reasons why were admirable. He was a complex thinker who truly cared about each word on the page and the different ways to present concepts. For me, the first edition of this book and the corresponding six-session videos were incredibly enlightening. My father, Jon Carlson, who had witnessed thousands of hours of taping psychotherapy sessions, shared with me that Jeremy's six sessions and the corresponding voice-over of Jeremy explaining his work in those sessions were among the best teaching tools he had ever created. I was so pleased that Jeremy's partner and spouse, Jennifer Hunter, stepped in to develop the second edition of this incredible book. Together, Jennifer and Jeremy do a masterful job of expanding people's knowledge about psychoanalysis beyond Freud into contemporary practice and modern times. And as with the first edition, my own knowledge base and appreciation for psychoanalytic thinking has deepened through my careful read of this book. I am certain that all readers will have the same experience.

# How to Use This Book
# With APA Psychotherapy Videos

Each book in the Theories of Psychotherapy Series is specifically paired with a video that demonstrates the theory applied in actual therapy with a real client. Many videos feature the author of the book as the guest therapist, allowing students to see an eminent scholar and practitioner putting the theory they write about into action.

The video programs have a number of features that make them excellent tools for learning more about theoretical concepts:

- Many video programs contain six full sessions of psychotherapy over time, giving viewers a chance to see how clients respond to the application of the theory over the course of several sessions.
- Each program has a brief introductory discussion recapping the basic features of the theory behind the approach demonstrated. This allows viewers to review the key aspects of the approach about which they have just read.
- The videos feature volunteer clients in unedited psychotherapy sessions. This provides a unique opportunity to get a sense of the look and feel of real psychotherapy, something that written case examples and transcripts sometimes cannot convey.

The books and videos together make a powerful teaching tool for showing how theoretical principles affect practice. In the case of this book, the video *Psychoanalytic Therapy Over Time*, which features the first author as the guest expert, provides a vivid example of how this approach looks in practice.

For more information, please visit APA Videos at https://www.apa.org/pubs/videos/

# Acknowledgments

Jeremy Safran, the sole author of the first edition of this book, left us in 2018. He was a beloved professor, therapist, mentor, friend, uncle, father, and my husband. As a singular thinker and theory savant, Jeremy was both the worst and the best choice to write a primer on psychoanalysis. He was a devotee of history, politics, philosophy, and religion. He was an expert in the theory of cognitive therapy, psychotherapy integration, emotion theory, psychotherapy research, and Buddhism as well as relational psychoanalysis. He conducted groundbreaking research on rupture and repair in the therapeutic relationship and wrote theoretical papers about will and agency, intersubjectivity, metacommunication, and the analytic relationship. He was the worst choice because he was a complex and contextual thinker who did not simplify psychoanalysis for the reader. This also made him the best choice. To practice psychoanalysis is to embrace ambiguity and complexity, to appreciate the political and social context of knowledge, and to accept the limits of what we can understand. Jeremy embodies these perspectives in this wonderful book as he did throughout his life. This book demonstrates his brilliance, generosity, clinical acuity, and personal honesty. The reissue is an opportunity to continue to offer these qualities to new generations of psychoanalytic students and extend his influence into the future.

I am infinitely grateful to the generous colleagues who shared their expertise to make this reissue possible: Paul Wachtel, Jessica Benjamin, Neil Altman, Howard Steele, Chris Muran, Steve Botticelli, Stan Messer, Catherine Eubanks, Joel Weinberger, Jill Bresler, Steve Reisner, Jennifer Hay, Kristen Peck. I also thank Joshua Maserow for his editorial support.

—Jennifer Hunter

# Psychoanalysis and Psychoanalytic Therapies

## Second Edition

# 1

# Introduction

Psychoanalysis has changed the way we think about our minds and what it means to be human. Its reach includes a groundbreaking form of psychological treatment, as well as models of psychological functioning, development, and psychopathology. Many divergent psycho-analytic theories and treatment modalities have been developed over more than a century through the writings of a host of different theorists and practitioners. Nonetheless, it is possible to speak in general terms about basic principles that cut across all psychoanalytic perspectives. These include (a) an assumption that all human beings are influenced by wishes, fantasies, or knowledge that is outside of awareness (*the unconscious*); (b) an interest in facilitating the awareness of unconscious motivations, thereby increasing choice; (c) an emphasis on exploring the ways in

As noted in the Acknowledgments, Jeremy Safran passed away in 2018 during early discussions for the revision of *Psychoanalysis and Psychoanalytic Therapies, Second Edition*, which was subsequently completed by Jennifer Hunter. As in the first edition, "I" statements are used throughout this book to represent Dr. Safran's perspective, voice, and work.

http://dx.doi.org/10.1037/0000190-001
*Psychoanalysis and Psychoanalytic Therapies, Second Edition*, by J. D. Safran and J. Hunter

which people avoid painful or threatening feelings, fantasies, and thoughts; (d) an assumption that people are ambivalent about change and an emphasis on the importance of exploring this ambivalence; (e) an emphasis on using the therapeutic relationship as an arena for exploring psychological processes and actions (both conscious and unconscious); (f) an emphasis on using the therapeutic relationship as an important vehicle of change; and (g) an emphasis on helping clients to understand the way in which their construction of their past and present plays a role in perpetuating habitual patterns.

In the early days of psychoanalysis, clients typically saw Freud and his colleagues four to six times per week, and treatment lasted from 6 weeks to 2 months. As the goals of psychoanalysis evolved from symptom reduction to more fundamental changes in personality functioning, the length of the average analysis gradually increased over time to the point at which it became common for an analysis to last 6 years or longer.

Many contemporary psychoanalysts still believe that long-term, intensive treatment has important advantages as a treatment modality. As the empirical evidence shows, although circumscribed symptoms can improve in short-term, less intensive therapy, more fundamental changes in personality functioning and underlying psychological structures take time (e.g., Howard, Kopta, Krause, & Orlinsky, 1986). Moreover, given that the client–therapist relationship is seen as a central mechanism of change, the theory holds that longer term, intensive treatment is necessary to allow this relationship to develop and play a transformative role. In contemporary psychoanalytic practice, it is common to see clients once or twice a week for a shorter term, but the basic analytic values and goals remain.

Psychoanalysis was the first modern Western system of psychotherapy, and most other forms of therapy evolved out of psychoanalysis, were strongly influence by it, or developed partially in reaction to it. The term *psychoanalysis* was originated by Sigmund Freud (1856–1939), a Viennese neurologist who with a number of key colleagues (e.g., Wilhelm Stekel, Paul Federn, Max Etington, Alfred Adler, Hans Sachs, Otto Rank,

Karl Abraham, Carl Jung, Sandor Ferenczi, Ernest Jones) developed a discipline that combined a form of psychological treatment with a model of psychological functioning, human development, and theory of change. The emergence of this discipline was influenced by a variety of developments taking place at the time in psychiatry, neurology, psychology, philosophy, and social and natural sciences. In addition, early psychoanalysis was influenced by Freud's attempts to defend against criticism from outside the field as well as dissenting perspectives and ideas raised by his own students and colleagues. Significant conflict lead to estrangement from many of his most important early colleagues as they developed their own divergent ideas; this group includes Jung, Rank, and Adler (Gay, 1988; Makari, 2008). Freud's theoretical perspective and ideas about psychoanalytic technique evolved over the course of his lifetime, and although his thinking is often presented as a unified and coherent system of thought, reading his articles and books is more like reading ongoing work in progress rather than a systematic and unified theory.

Although Freud undeniably was the single most influential figure in the initial development of psychoanalysis, many other creative thinkers played a role in its development from the very beginning. Some of their ideas led Freud to sharpen his thinking in response, some of their ideas were assimilated and modified by Freud in various ways, and some of their ideas were not assimilated by Freud but had a subsequent impact on their own students' thinking and on future generations of psychoanalysts (Makari, 2008). Although psychoanalysis began with Freud's writing and lectures and the early writing of a small group of colleagues around him in Vienna, by the time of Freud's death in 1939, it was becoming an international movement with important centers in Vienna, Zurich, Berlin, Budapest, Italy, France, England, the United States, and Latin America. Each of these centers contributed its unique influence to the development of psychoanalysis, and a host of different schools and theories of psychoanalysis have evolved in different countries since 1939 (Makari, 2008). Adherents to different traditions within psychoanalysis interpret Freud differently and can disagree about major premises and technical recommendations.

## PSYCHOANALYSIS TODAY

Although it is understandable for critics to equate psychoanalysis with Freud, it is important to recognize that the value of psychoanalytic treatment and the validity of psychoanalytic theory are not tied to the validity of Freud's thinking. Freud was one person writing from a particular historical and cultural place. Some of his ideas were more valid in their original historical and cultural context than they are in contemporary times, and some were flawed from the beginning. As readers will see, there are some dramatic differences between early psychoanalysis and the form it has today. Relative to Freud's time, contemporary American psychoanalysis has a greater emphasis on the mutuality of the therapeutic relationship; an emphasis on the fundamentally human nature of the therapeutic relationship; more of an emphasis on flexibility, creativity, and spontaneity in the therapeutic process; and a more optimistic perspective on life and human nature. Contrary to common belief, there is actually substantial and growing empirical support for the effectiveness of psychoanalytically oriented treatments (Leichsenring, Luyten, et al., 2015; Levy, Ablon, & Kaechele, 2012; Shedler, 2010) and the validity of various psychoanalytic constructs (Westen, 1998; Westen & Gabbard, 1999). And there has been a growing emphasis on adapting psychoanalytic theory and practice in a culturally and politically responsive fashion (Altman, 2010; Aron & Starr, 2012; Gutwill & Hollander, 2006; Perez Foster, Moskowitz, & Javier, 1996).

In the United States, psychoanalysis has evolved under the influence of certain characteristic American attitudes, including a tendency toward optimism and the philosophy of American egalitarianism. Another important factor is that many of today's leading analysts came of age during the cultural revolution in the 1970s—a time when traditional social norms and sources of authority were being challenged. In addition, prominent feminist psychoanalytic thinkers have challenged many of the patriarchal assumptions implicit in traditional psychoanalytic theory, raised important questions about the dynamics of power in the therapeutic relationship, and reformulated psychoanalytic thinking about gender (e.g., Benjamin, 1988, 1995, 2018; Dimen, 2003; Harris, 2008). Another influence has been a postmodern sensibility that challenges the assumption that one can ever come to know reality objectively, maintains a skeptical attitude toward universalizing truth claims, and emphasizes the importance of theoretical pluralism. A final influence has been an influx of clinical psychologists, social workers, people of color, women, and people with diverse gender identities and sexual orientations into postgraduate psychoanalytic training institutes in the past few decades. This has led to significant and intellectually interesting changes in a discipline that was traditionally dominated by White male psychiatrists.

Unfortunately, many in the broader mental health field and the general public are unaware of these changes within psychoanalysis and are responding to a partial or caricatured understanding of the tradition on the basis of aspects of psychoanalytic theory, practice, and attitude that are no longer prominent. Although there are many valid critiques of psychoanalysis in both its past and current forms, I believe that the current marginalization of psychoanalysis is partially attributable to certain contemporary cultural biases, especially in the United States, that are not unequivocally healthy ones. These biases include an emphasis on optimism, speed, pragmatism, instrumentality, and an intolerance of ambiguity. Although all of these emphases certainly have their value, they can underestimate the complexity of human nature and the difficulty of the change process. American culture tends to gloss over the more tragic dimensions of life, to espouse the belief that we can all be happy if we try hard enough, and to be biased toward a "quick-fix mentality." Psychoanalysis originated in continental Europe—in a culture that had experienced centuries of poverty; oppression of the masses by the ruling classes; ongoing religious conflict and oppression; and generations of warfare culminating in two world wars that were unprecedented in scale, degree of devastation, and tragedy.

Although American psychoanalysis tends to be more optimistic and pragmatic than its European counterpart, it still retains many of the traditional psychoanalytic values, such as the appreciation of human complexity, a recognition that contentment is not necessarily the same as a two-dimensional version of "happiness," and a recognition that change is not always easy or quick. Additionally, there has been movement in contemporary psychoanalysis toward recovering some of the culturally subversive, socially progressive, and politically engaged spirit that was once more characteristic of the discipline. My hope is that this book will both correct misconceptions about traditional psychoanalysis and introduce some of the more important recent developments in psychoanalytic theory and practice. This will be done through discussion of current theoretical developments and the use of clinical examples that demonstrate current clinical practice. In the latter, the client names and identities have been disguised throughout the book.

## THE TENSION BETWEEN CONFORMIST AND SUBVERSIVE THREADS IN PSYCHOANALYSIS

For many years, psychoanalysis was the dominant theory for mental health practitioners in the United States and many other countries. From the late 1960s until the present time, however, psychoanalysis in the United States has become increasingly marginalized within both the health care system and clinical training programs. There are reasons for the declining fortunes of psychoanalysis. One important factor is that during its heyday, psychoanalysis earned a reputation as a conservative cultural force with a tendency toward orthodoxy, insularity, arrogance, and elitism. It also earned a reputation as a somewhat esoteric discipline with a limited interest in grappling with the concrete problems that many people deal with in their everyday lives and a limited appreciation of the social and political factors that affect their lives. Instead, psychoanalysis came to be seen by many as a self-indulgent pastime for the financially comfortable.

The fact that psychoanalysis came to earn this reputation is ironic. Although Freud initially began developing psychoanalysis as a treatment for clients presenting with symptoms that other physicians were unable to treat, his ambitions and the ambitions of subsequent psychoanalysts ultimately extended beyond the realm of therapy into social theory and cultural critique. Freud and many early analysts had medical backgrounds. Nevertheless, Freud came to feel strongly that psychoanalysis should not become a medical subspecialty and, in fact, prized the cultural and intellectual breadth that could be brought to the field by analysts with diverse education backgrounds and intellectual interests. Many early analysts, including Freud, were members of an emerging, educated Jewish middle class whose upward social mobility was made possible by the open, politically progressive policies of the Austro-Hungarian Empire at the turn of the century and who contributed to the development of this culture.

The early analysts thus tended to be members of a liberal, progressive intelligentsia—a traditionally oppressed and marginalized group. They aspired toward social acceptance but at the same time tended to regard prevailing cultural assumptions from a critical perspective. This critical and in some respects subversive stance went hand in hand with a vision of progressive social transformation. Psychoanalysis began in part as a radical critique of the illness-producing effects of social suppression and consequent psychological repression of sexuality. Freud was deeply interested in broad social and cultural concerns. He was critical of various trappings of the physician's privilege, and until the end of his life he supported free psychoanalytic clinics, stood up for the flexible fee, and defended the practice of psychoanalysis by professionals without medical training. Many of the early analysts were progressive social activists committed to political critique and social justice. Sandor Ferenczi, one of Freud's closest colleagues, critiqued social hypocrisy and conventionalism, founded a free clinic in Budapest, and passionately defended the rights of women and homosexuals. In Berlin in the 1920s, Karl Abraham, Ernst Simmel, and Max Etington set up a public psychoanalytic clinic that became a bastion of social and political progressivism (Danto, 2005). A number of these analysts were influenced by left wing socialist thinking. This is not surprising given that they came of age in the politically charged culture of Vienna and Berlin, where the Marxist critique of capitalism was widely discussed in intellectual circles. They viewed themselves as brokers of social change and saw psychoanalysis as a challenge to conventional political codes and as more of a social mission than a medical discipline. Prominent analysts such as Wilhelm Reich (1941), Erich Fromm (1941), and Otto Fenichel (1945), among others, were well known for their socialist or Marxist commitments and their fusion of psychoanalysis and social concerns.

This subversive trend stands in contrast to the "professionalization" of psychoanalysis in the United States, by which it became increasingly conservative and conformist. During the early decades of the 20th century, when psychoanalysis was beginning to take root in the United States, the medical community was struggling to upgrade and standardize physician training. In 1938, a fateful decision was made early by the American Psychoanalytic Association to restrict formal psychoanalytic training to physicians. A concern about protecting the professionalism of psychoanalysis played a role in developing a purist, elitist, and rigid form of psychoanalysis with a veneer of scientific respectability, a discouragement of innovation, and a tendency toward social conservatism. As psychoanalysis became established as a subspecialty of medicine, the social prestige of the psychoanalytic profession grew as well. Chairs in most major psychiatry departments were psychoanalysts, and most psychiatry residency training programs provided at least some training in psychoanalytically oriented treatment.

The United States became the center of the psychoanalytic world, and massive amounts of time, effort, and money went into psychoanalytic training and the development of the profession. Psychoanalysis became a lucrative, high-prestige, and socially conservative profession, attracting candidates who often had an interest in becoming respected members of the establishment rather than in challenging it (Jacoby, 1983; McWilliams, 2004). Unlike the original psychoanalysts in Europe coming from backgrounds and educational systems that were intellectually rich and scholarly in nature, many of the candidates entering psychoanalytic training in the United States came from educational systems that were technical in nature. There was a tendency for psychoanalysis to be applied as a narrow, technical approach with rather inflexible ideas about correct and incorrect technique, analogous to the way one tends to think of medical procedures.

Over 50 years ago, Robert Knight, then president of the American Psychoanalytic Association, remarked on the more "conventional" character of the psychoanalytic candidates of his era, relative to the more original and individualistic character of the candidates of the 1920s and 1930s. According to Knight (1953), the psychoanalytic candidates of the 1950s were "not so introspective, are inclined to read only the literature that is assigned and wish to get through with the training requirements as soon as possible" (p. 218).

In addition, medical education, with its traditional respect for hierarchy and authority, tended to infuse the training of psychoanalysts with a sensibility that led to an unquestioning acceptance of the words of one's teachers rather than to the development of a critical and reflective spirit. And this same sensibility tended to color the therapist–client relationship in a way that institutionalized and exacerbated the inherent power imbalance in the therapeutic relationship instead of encouraging a more democratic egalitarian relationship (Jacoby, 1983; Moskowitz, 1996).

Meanwhile, various forces at play were about to lead to dramatic changes in American psychoanalysis. With the rise of biological psychiatry and the explosion in the development of new psychotropic medications, psychoanalysis became less favored within American psychiatry. The publication of the *Diagnostic and Statistical Manual of Mental Disorders* (*DSM*; third ed.; American Psychiatric Association, 1980), which attempted to purge the *DSM* of psychoanalytic thinking, further contributed to the growing marginalization of American psychoanalysis (e.g., Horowitz, 2003). Training curricula within psychiatry residencies shifted away from introducing residents to the basics of psychoanalytic theory and practice, and the number of psychiatry residents applying for training in psychoanalytic institutes decreased dramatically over time.

Around this time, the Division of Psychoanalysis (Division 39) formed within the American Psychological Association. In 1986, Division 39 filed a class action suit against the American Psychoanalytic Association, arguing that the refusal to admit psychologists as candidates within psychoanalytic training institutes was a violation of the antitrust regulations because, by establishing a monopoly of the field of psychoanalysis by physicians, it was preventing fair competition for clients by psychologists and depriving them of their livelihood. Ironically, by the time the lawsuit was settled, market forces were already opening the doors of psychoanalytic training institutes to psychologists, because as the number of candidates seeking psychoanalytic training continued to dwindle, traditional institutes became eager to recruit psychologists (McWilliams, 2004; Moskowitz, 1996).

In the past 30 years, many of the more significant and innovative contributors to the development of American psychoanalytic theory have been psychologists. Psychologists have become the torchbearers for psychoanalysis in this country. This new breed of psychoanalytic theorist and researcher has played a vital role in transforming psychoanalysis into a less insular and more intellectually vital discipline, grounded in an appreciation of contemporary developments in a broad range of social sciences, including psychology, sociology, political science, and philosophy. The revitalizing influence of psychology on psychoanalysis is attributable to certain factors. First, there is more of an emphasis in clinical psychology training programs on the development of critical-thinking skills, in contrast to residency training in psychiatry, which places a greater emphasis on memorization of facts and technical mastery. Moreover, training in psychology does place more emphasis on the study of basic psychological, developmental, cultural, and social processes that are relevant to understanding both psychopathology and the process of change. In addition, psychologists receive more training in empirical research methodology than do psychiatrists. Although this does not necessarily lead psychologists to maintain empirical research programs after going into psychoanalytic training, it does help to hone their critical thinking skills and to deepen their appreciation of the limits of various theoretical constructs.

Another important variable influences the changing character of American psychoanalysis. Given that pursuing formal psychoanalytic training in today's culture is less likely to be a pathway to professional prestige or financial success, the typical candidate is more likely to be drawn to the field for intrinsic reasons. Especially given the increasingly marginal status of psychoanalysis within the general culture and within mainstream clinical psychology, those attracted to the field are less likely to buy into prevailing cultural and professional values and assumptions and are more likely to have a critical perspective. Thus, ironically, the marginalization of psychoanalysis provides a potential catalyst for innovative thinking. In this respect, important aspects of the emerging sensibility in contemporary American psychoanalysis may be closer in nature to the sensibility of the early psychoanalysts than that of American psychoanalysis during the mid-20th century.

## PSYCHOANALYSIS VERSUS PSYCHODYNAMIC THERAPY

Traditionally, psychoanalysts have made a clear distinction between *psychoanalysis* and what is referred to as *psychoanalytic* or *psychodynamic therapy*. The term *psychoanalysis* has been reserved for a form of treatment with certain defining characteristics or parameters. The term *psychodynamic therapy* has been used to refer to forms of treatment that are based on psychoanalytic theory but that lack some of the defining characteristics of psychoanalysis. Over the years there has been some controversy over which parameters of psychoanalysis are defining criteria and which are not. A common stance has been that psychoanalysis is long term, intensive (e.g., a minimum of three sessions per week), and open ended (i.e., no fixed termination date or number of sessions). In addition, traditional psychoanalysis came to be characterized by a specific therapist stance that involves refraining from giving the client advice or being overly directive, maintaining anonymity by reducing the amount of information one provides about one's personal life or one's feeling and reactions in the session, attempting to maintain the stance of the neutral party by speaking sparsely, and having the client recline on a couch while the therapist sits upright, out of view of the client. This traditional conceptualization of some of the key characteristics of psychoanalysis came to be known as *classical psychoanalysis.*

# HOW DID THE DISTINCTION BETWEEN PSYCHOANALYSIS AND PSYCHODYNAMIC THERAPY EMERGE?

In the 20th century, psychoanalysts in the United States often asserted that only those within the milder range of pathology were suitable for analysis. They would speak of a client in terms of their "analyzability," referring to their ability to tolerate and benefit from intensive analytic work. Over time, analysts have experimented with treating a broader range of clients than had initially been the case. As a result, it became necessary to modify various treatment parameters to adapt the approach to clients with different characteristics and needs. Some clients find it too threatening, anxiety provoking, or destabilizing to explore their unconscious motivation and benefit more from structure, advice, and help with problem solving. Some require active reassurance and find the therapist's reluctance to provide direction or exert direct influence too frustrating or anxiety provoking. Some feel uncomfortable lying on a couch and experience it as a form of submission to the therapist. Some do not have the time or the financial resources to attend frequent sessions per week or long-term treatment. To adapt to the needs of these clients, therapists experimented with modifying all of these parameters. These modified versions of psychoanalysis came to be termed *psychodynamic therapies.* This has resulted in inevitable tensions within the professional communities over what can be considered "pure psychoanalysis."

Although it is premature to say that debates of this kind have ceased, I think it is fair to say that many psychoanalysts no longer make such rigid distinctions. Practitioners today often use the term *psychoanalysis* to refer to a depth-oriented treatment performed by a trained analyst, irrespective of frequency or the fine points of technique. My own perspective is that although the distinction between psychoanalysis and psychodynamic or psychoanalytic treatment has more to do with the politics of the discipline and professional elitism than any theoretically justifiable criteria, it is a mistake to assume that all of the parameters associated with a traditional psychoanalysis are outdated. There is often an important trade-off with these decisions of technique. For example, the traditional analytic stance of attempting to maintain anonymity can alienate clients, especially in contemporary American culture, which tends to be less formal and hierarchical. At the same time, less explicit discussion of the analyst's thoughts and feelings can leave more room for the client's associations, including assumptions about the analyst that may be informed by transference. Many clients really do need and value advice and active feedback, but too much advice can interfere with clients' ability to develop their own resources and perpetuate a stance of helplessness. Some clients benefit from short-term treatment, but many really do need longer treatment.

Many analysts have found that using the couch facilitates therapeutic processes, such as helping clients to direct their attention inwards toward more important experiences that are subtle in nature and less accessible. It may be easier to free associate without looking to the analyst for a reaction. However, I feel that there are treatments or times in a treatment when an ongoing process of face-to-face encounter between the therapist and client plays a central role in the change process. For example, if the client comes to treatment with problems in intimacy, the ability to explore the quality of emotional contact between the therapist and client on a moment-by-moment basis can be important. It can also be critical for the therapist to be able to see the client's face to develop a nuanced sense of what he or she is feeling and to be able to attune empathically. Or it may be important for the client to have face-to-face contact with the therapist to be able to gauge his ongoing emotional reactions. Psychoanalysts are increasingly viewing the process of ongoing mutual affective regulation between client and therapist as an important change process. This process is facilitated when there is visual contact between the two and they are able to engage in an ongoing process of mutual responsiveness to each other's affective experience.

# 2

# History

Sigmund Freud was born in 1856 into a relatively poor but upwardly mobile Jewish family in a small town in what was then the Austro-Hungarian Empire, approximately 150 miles from Vienna. Despite his broad interests growing up, he eventually chose to study medicine, in part because of the allure of science as a possible road to fame and prestige combined with optimism about science as the ultimate path to knowledge. Freud's development of psychoanalytic theory and practice was influenced by a number of cultural and intellectual trends and scientific models that dominated European circles in the late 19th and early 20th centuries (Gay, 1988; Makari, 2008, 2015). One important foundation for Freud's more abstract theoretical ideas can be found in the dominant tradition in German neurology during Freud's medical training, which was based on the belief that all psychological phenomena could be understood in neurophysiologic and mechanistic terms. This emphasis

http://dx.doi.org/10.1037/0000190-002
*Psychoanalysis and Psychoanalytic Therapies, Second Edition*, by J. D. Safran and J. Hunter

on grounding psychology in neurophysiology remained a key influence in Freud's thinking throughout his life. Although prescient in his anticipation of today's booming interest and remarkable developments in neuropsychology and the brain sciences, many of the dominant neurophysiological models of Freud's era are considered outdated by contemporary scientific standards. Freud's effort to synthesize psychology with developments that were current in the fields of biology and neurophysiology played a central role in the formulation of what is referred to as his *drive theory* of motivation. In drive theory, Freud assumed that human beings are fundamentally asocial in nature and that the primary motivation is to maintain psychic energy at a constant level. Psychic energy is, for Freud, a force that lies on the boundary between the physical and biological and that drives or propels intrapsychic processes and action. According to Freud, once psychic energy is activated (through either an internal or external event), there is a need to discharge it in order to maintain a constant level of psychic energy in the system. This discharge can take place in various ways (e.g., becoming preoccupied with a person, an idea, or a fantasy, or the eruption of symptoms).

Another formative influence on Freud's early thinking, acquired in his time studying in Paris with renowned French neurologist Jean-Martin Charcot, was his exposure to what were then recent developments in French neurology and psychiatry that were beginning to explore the role that the splitting of consciousness can play in psychopathology (Gay, 1988). Charcot had established an international reputation through his use of hypnosis (or what was referred to as *mesmerism*) with hysterics. *Hysterics* were clients who presented with a variety of dramatic physical problems that could not be accounted for on an organic basis. These clients tended to complain of problems such as paralysis of the limbs, blindness, deafness, and physical convulsions (Gay, 1988). Today, this particular pattern of symptom presentation and the associated diagnosis are much less common.

Freud returned to Vienna as a proponent of Charcot, and he began to synthesize French and German influences on his thinking. Subsequently, Freud was to build on and then critique Charcot's position. In 1886, Freud began collaborating with an older colleague, Josef Breuer, a mentor and patron of Freud's when Freud was in medical school. Breuer was a highly respected physician in Vienna known for his dramatic successes treating clients with hysteria. His approach involved encouraging them to talk about themselves and helping them to remember traumatic experiences in their lives that they had forgotten. Breuer found that when these clients were able to recall these experiences in an affectively charged fashion, their symptoms would diminish.

Freud and Breuer came to believe that hysterical symptoms were the result of suppressed affect or emotional experience that had been cut off at the time of the trauma and thus had to express itself in the form of physical symptoms. Freud came to believe that by using hypnotic techniques to help clients recover memories of the trauma and to experience associated affect that had been suppressed at the time, the client could be cured. In the period from 1893 to 1895, Breuer and Freud published *Studies in Hysteria* together—a book consisting of a number of case histories and a theoretical section outlining their current thinking about the psychological origins of hysteria (Breuer & Freud, 1893–1895/1955).

By the time *Studies of Hysteria* was published, however, Freud was already distancing himself from Breuer, whom he felt he had outgrown, and Freud had begun to refine both his thinking and treatment of hysteria (Makari, 2008). At first Freud believed that most neurotic symptoms were attributable to a history of childhood sexual abuse, a perspective that Breuer did not share. Over time, Freud shifted his view to believe that although sexual abuse could play a role in the development of psychological problems, recovered memories of sexual abuse were often partially constructed and reflected unconscious or repressed childhood sexual fantasies propelled by sexual instincts (Gay, 1988; Makari, 2008).

At the turn of the century, Freud began to pursue a long-standing interest in the role of dreams as a potential window into unconscious aspects of the human psyche. Freud's (1900/1953) publication of *The Interpretation of Dreams* eventually caught the attention of the highly respected Eugene Bleuler, the director of the Burgholzli Institute in Zurich. The Burgholzli Hospital (which specialized in the treatment of patients with schizophrenia) was widely known and respected throughout Western Europe as a prominent medical and scientific establishment. Bleuler had a number of talented young psychiatrists on his staff, including Carl Jung. Under Bleuler's guidance, Jung was already establishing an important reputation in the scientific community for adapting research methodology from experimental psychology to study unconscious processes through word association tests. Bleuler encouraged Jung to read Freud, and an alliance started to develop between Freud, Jung, Bleuler, and the group of psychiatrists in Zurich working with Bleuler. Because of the prominence of Bleuler and his colleagues within mainstream psychiatry, this alliance ultimately played a critical role in contributing to the acceptance of psychoanalysis in scientific circles throughout Western Europe (Makari, 2008).

In 1909, Freud and Jung were invited by the American psychologist Stanley Hall to give a series of lectures at Clark University in Worcester, Massachusetts. The lectures were well attended and warmly received by prominent American intellectuals, psychiatrists, neurologists, and psychologists. This warm reception laid the ground for the subsequent assimilation of psychoanalysis by American culture and ultimately for the transformation of the United States into one of the most important centers of psychoanalysis in the world (Gay, 1988; Hale, 1971, 1995; Makari, 2008). The years leading up to World War II and the ultimate declaration of war in 1939 were to have a profound effect on the lives of most psychoanalysts living in continental Europe and on the development of psychoanalysis. In Germany, the growing influence of Nazism led to the persecution of vast numbers of continental analysts who were Jewish. Those who had the good fortune to escape immigrated to countries throughout the world. The United States was the most common destination, but both England and Latin America became desirable locations as well. All three regions developed into important centers for psychoanalysis that ultimately led to a growing number of theoretical and technical innovations in psychoanalytic thought influenced in different ways by different cultures over time (Gay, 1988; Makari, 2008). In the United States, the military began relying heavily on psychoanalytically oriented psychiatrists and psychologists to conduct psychological assessments and treat psychologically traumatized soldiers, and this had a massive impact on the growth of American psychoanalysis (Hale, 1995).

## THE EVOLUTION OF EARLY PSYCHOANALYTIC THINKING

In this section, I briefly summarize the evolution of early psychoanalytic theory from the late 1890s to the mid-1920s. I begin with Freud's early use of hypnosis to help patients recover traumatic memories, and I continue on to discuss the innovation of fundamental psychoanalytic principles such as free association, resistance, and transference. By 1923 Freud had developed his foundational structural model of the mind, which distinguishes between three psychic agencies: the id, the ego, and the superego.

### Free Association

Although Freud's early forays into psychoanalysis used mesmerism or hypnosis to help clients recover lost memories and associated emotions, over time he found this technique to be unreliable. Although some clients were good candidates for hypnosis, many were simply not sufficiently suggestible. Instead of hypnotizing his clients, Freud began to encourage them to "say everything that comes to mind without censoring." This was the origin of the psychoanalytic principle of free association, in which clients are encouraged to attempt to suspend their self-critical function and verbalize fantasies, images, associations, and feelings that are on the edge of awareness.

Over time Freud and the early analysts came to believe that it was vital to make a clear distinction between psychoanalysis and the tradition of hypnosis out of which it had emerged. In addition to the unreliability of hypnotic techniques, Freud came to distrust the accuracy of many recovered memories. Freud and his colleagues were eager to establish psychoanalysis as a treatment that was based on scientific principles. There was a growing sense that one of the important values of psychoanalysis involved the pursuit of truth. Hypnosis helps people through suggestion or through fostering a certain type of belief. In contrast, the goal of psychoanalysis was to help people become more skeptical and face uncomfortable truths about themselves. Psychoanalysis did not involve indoctrination to any particular ideas but rather was a counterindoctrination against cultural and social beliefs and judgments (Reiff, 1966).

This emphasis on distinguishing psychoanalysis from suggestion came to exert an important influence on early thinking about both the mechanisms of change and preferred interventions. With respect to the mechanisms of change, emphasis was placed on insight and understanding as the curative factors, and the impact of more human qualities of the therapist and the relational factors were downplayed. The key intervention was the analyst's interpretation, which exposed the client to aspects of his or her unconscious that had been out of awareness. Advice, suggestion, reassurance, and encouragement were discouraged because they blurred the boundaries between the truth-seeking aspects of psychoanalysis and the element of suggestion, and they could potentially compromise the client's autonomy by encouraging dependence on the analyst.

## Resistance

Freud discovered that his clients were not always able to follow his instructions to free associate. This led to the development of the notion of *resistance*, which was understood as the client's reluctance or inability to collaborate with the therapist in the prescribed fashion. This difficulty is hardly surprising considering that analysands were being asked to face aspects of themselves that were being kept out of awareness. Facing these inner experiences could invoke intrapsychic pain, shame, or disorganizing confusion. At first, Freud used his authority as the doctor to pressure clients to overcome their resistance and say whatever came to mind regardless of their tendency toward self-censorship. Subsequently, he and other analysts came to believe that the therapeutic exploration of the resistance was a vitally important therapeutic task in and of itself.

## Transference

A third noteworthy stage in the ongoing evolution of Freud's thinking was the development of the concept of *transference*. Freud observed that it was not uncommon for his clients to view him and relate to him in ways that were reminiscent of the way they viewed and related to significant figures in their childhoods—especially their parents. He thus speculated that they were "transferring" a template from the past onto the present situation. For example, a client with a tyrannical father might begin to see the therapist as tyrannical.

At first Freud saw this transference as an impediment to treatment. He speculated that it was a form of resistance to remembering traumatic experiences. The idea was that the client would act out the previous relationship in the therapeutic setting rather than remember it. Over time, however, Freud came to see the development of the transference as an indispensable part of the psychoanalytic process. By reliving the past in the analytic relationship, the client provided the therapist with an opportunity to help him or her develop an understanding of how past relationships were influencing the experience of the present in an emotionally immediate way. This conceptualization of the potential value of transference provided additional justification of the therapist retaining a neutral and uninvolved stance. The idea emerged that the analyst, by maintaining a certain degree of anonymity (through withholding information about his or her own life or personal reactions), could function as a blank screen that would encourage the development of the transference and decrease the possibility that it would be contaminated by the therapist's real characteristics.

## The Abandonment of Seduction Theory

In his early writing, Freud contended that early sexual trauma was often the root of psychological symptoms. Over time he came to abandon his earlier theory that all of his clients had been sexually abused as children (the seduction theory) and instead developed the theory of infantile sexuality and instinctual drives. Consistent with the work of sexuality researchers of his time, such as Havelock Ellis and Albert Moll, Freud began to believe, in contrast to the common view that childhood is a time of sexual innocence, that children actually experience sexual or at least presexual feelings from the beginning and that these stem from instinctual sources (Makari, 2008). Freud came to believe that these presexual feelings lead children to have fantasies about having sexual encounters with adults. As children mature, these fantasies are repressed because they are experienced as threatening. Freud speculated that often memories of sexual trauma are actually the product of reconstructed memories that are based on childhood sexual fantasies, related to the sexual drive, rather than real sexual trauma. So as the emphasis of his work changed to the role of the unconscious and of fantasy, he felt that internal conflict over sexual feelings was the real cause of neurotic problems, although he never discounted the possibility of actual early trauma.

This shift away from the seduction theory to an emphasis on unconscious fantasy is controversial when viewed from a contemporary perspective in relation to issues of recovered memories of sexual abuse. For many years the actual incidence of childhood sexual abuse was minimized in the psychiatric literature, and survivors were not believed. Given the current recognition that child sexual abuse is much more common than it was once thought to be, Freud's shift in emphasis from seduction theory to drive theory can be seen as bolstering this denial. In addition, Freud's growing emphasis on the role that endogenous drives play in the development of emotional problems led to a neglect of the role that environmental factors, such as the quality of caretaking, play in the developmental process. Although this neglect has been remedied in most contemporary psychoanalytic theories, it has been the source of understandable critique by feminist writers and advocates for survivors of childhood abuse.

## The Development of Structural Theory

In 1923, Freud published *The Ego and the Id*, which lays out the foundations for what subsequently became known as his structural theory

(Freud, 1923/1961). In this paper, he distinguished between three psychic agencies: the id, the ego, and the superego. The id is the aspect of the psyche that is instinctually based and present from birth. The id presses for immediate instinctual gratification without any regard for realistic concerns about the realities of the immediate situation. The superego is the psychic agency that emerges through the internalization of societal values and norms, which would be in conflict with the gratification of id desires. The ego represents the concerns of reality and helps the individual to reconcile the id and superego. It is thus more rational in nature. For example, the id presses for immediate sexual gratification, the superego opposes gratification of that desire, and the ego allows the individual to delay instinctual gratification or to find ways of channeling instinctual needs in a socially acceptable fashion (e.g., skillfully seducing the object of one's sexual desire or redirecting one's sexual desire in a more appropriate direction). The superego often becomes overly harsh and demanding and can lead to self-destructive feelings of guilt and a punitive and rejecting stance toward one's own instinctual needs and wishes. One of the goals of analysis has been to help the individual become more aware of the overly harsh nature of his superego so that he becomes less self-punitive.

When the instinctually derived wishes that begin to emerge are experienced as dangerous because they are incompatible with the demands of the superego, the ego signals their presence with anxiety. This anxiety triggers the use of various psychic processes to keep the wishes, fantasies, and associated feelings out of awareness. These psychic processes, which are referred to as defenses, are discussed in detail later. A fundamental premise emerges out of this structural perspective: there is an ongoing dynamic tension between instinctually derived wishes and defenses against them. When this tension or conflict is managed in a relatively healthy way, the individual is able to be sufficiently aware of both his needs and wishes and the anxieties they evoke and to find a constructive and adaptive way of negotiating this tension. However, when this conflict is managed in a maladaptive way, psychological symptoms can result.

## PSYCHOANALYSIS BEYOND FREUD

By the time of Freud's death in 1939, several psychoanalytic traditions were beginning to emerge, influenced by a number of seminal theorists writing in a range of different countries and cultural traditions. In this section, I briefly review some of these traditions, including ego psychology, Kleinian and post-Kleinian theory, object relations theory, interpersonal psychoanalysis, relational psychoanalysis, and Lacanian psychoanalysis.

### The Development of Ego Psychology in Britain and the United States

Freud's structural theory and some of the theoretical developments in his thinking that led up to it ultimately gave rise to an important tradition of psychoanalysis that came to be known as *ego psychology*. Ego psychology focuses on the ego's normal and pathological development, its handling of libidinal and aggressive impulses, and its adaptation to reality. From this perspective, neurotic symptoms are examined as a compromise between impulses and defenses against those impulses. For example, a fear of knives could be seen as an ego-mediated defense, informed by the prohibitions of the superego, against an id-dictated aggressive drive to hurt others. Treatment relies heavily on defense analysis; the aim is to help patients understand their own use of defenses so that they can accept their own desires and make freer choices.

The unofficial leader of the ego psychology tradition was Freud's daughter, Anna Freud, who moved to London in 1938 with her father, 1 year before he died. Under the influence of analysts such as Anna Freud (1936), Wilhelm Reich (1941), and Otto Fenichel (1945), ego psychological thinking emerged and placed considerable emphasis on the need for understanding and interpreting the defensive functioning of the ego in order to find a way of exploring unconscious drives, fantasies, or wishes.

In the United States, the European émigré Heinz Hartmann (1964) became one of the key figures in another strand of ego psychology that was invested in broadening psychoanalysis beyond a psychotherapeutic tradition into a more general theory of psychological development and psychic functioning. Hartmann and his colleagues were particularly interested in the adaptive aspects of the ego and in the investigation of the various ways in which the ego helps the individual adapt to reality. Ego psychology became the dominant tradition of psychoanalysis in North America at that time.

Some of the most significant, clinically relevant American psychoanalytic writing of the time came out of the New York Psychoanalytic Institute and was synthesized and articulated by Jacob Arlow and Charles Brenner in particular (e.g., Arlow & Brenner, 1964). Arlow and Brenner (1964) emphasized the ubiquity of intrapsychic conflict in all aspects of the individual's functioning. For example, whereas Hartman argued that aspects of the ego are sufficiently independent of the id to be completely rational and conflict free, Arlow and Brenner argued that all aspects of the individual's functioning must be understood as compromises between underlying unconscious, instinctually based wishes and defenses against them.

## The Development of Kleinian and Object Relations Theory in Britain

A second major psychoanalytic tradition emerging out of some of Freud's more mature thinking came to be known as *object relations theory*. When Anna Freud and her father arrived in London in 1938, there was already an influential British school of psychoanalysis emerging under the leadership of the Austrian émigré Melanie Klein (1882–1960). Klein, who had been analyzed by Freud's close colleagues Sandor Ferenczi (1873–1933) and Karl Abraham (1949), had immigrated to London in 1926. Originally a child analyst, Klein was particularly interested in understanding the early relationship between the mother and the infant, and her theory laid the groundwork for understanding how psychological maturation involves developing internal representations of our relationships with significant others. Klein's thinking also set the foundation for subsequent theoretical developments in psychoanalysis that viewed human beings as fundamentally interpersonal creatures who have a evolutionarily based relationship to the mother and to other human beings.

Object relations theory emphasizes how our internal representations of early relationships influence the way in which we both choose romantic partners and friends and experience others. These internal representations are referred to as *internal objects* or *internal object relations*. Much of the writing about the process through which internal objects or internal object relations are developed (a process referred to as *internalization*), although clinically rich, is conceptually complicated and can be ambiguous and difficult to grasp (Eagle, 1984; Schafer, 1968).

Once Anna Freud arrived in London and began the process of establishing her own power base, the theoretical rivalries between Kleinians and Freudians became intense and vitriolic, threatening the survival of the relatively new British Psychoanalytic Society. During a series of what were characterized as "controversial discussions," Freudians critiqued many of the central Kleinian ideas. These discussions revolved around critiques of fundamental Kleinian assumptions such as the degree to which elaborate unconscious fantasies can be attributed to infants and the Kleinian tendency to emphasize interpretations of deep unconscious fantasies in both children and adult clients, without an adequate exploration of defenses that are closer to the client's conscious awareness. These discussions (or more accurately, heated debates) ultimately led to further clarifications in both Kleinian and Freudian thinking.

A so-called gentleman's agreement was forged between the Freudians and Kleinians in which it was agreed that the two traditions would coexist within the British Psychoanalytic Society. Throughout the 1940s and 1950s, some of the more innovative theoretical and technical work emerged out of the work of Klein and her followers, who became particularly interested in working with difficult treatment-resistant cases. Some of the more prominent Kleinian analysts who emerged during this period included theorists such as Hannah Segal, Herbert Rosenfeld, Joan Riviere, Susan Isaacs, Esther Bick, and Wilfred Bion (for a review, see, e.g., Sayers, 2001).

A third group of psychoanalytic theorists emerging out of the British Psychoanalytic Society consisted of analysts who were influenced by both Freudian and Kleinian ideas but were unwilling to formally align themselves politically with either tradition. These analysts, who became known as the British Independents or the Middle Group, consisted of theorists such as Ronald Fairbairn, Michael Balint, Donald Winnicott, Marion Milner, Masud Khan, and John Bowlby (for an excellent survey of the British Independent tradition, see Rayner, 1991). Some of the key qualities associated with the work of these Middle Group analysts were an emphasis on the importance of spontaneity, creativity, and therapist flexibility and the value of providing clients with a supportive and nurturing environment. Many developments coming out of the Kleinian and Middle Group traditions have subsequently been assimilated into more recent developments in American psychoanalysis. Winnicott (1958, 1965) in particular has become an important inspiration to many contemporary North American psychoanalysts who place an important emphasis on creativity, spontaneity, and authenticity. And John Bowlby's work has given rise to the extremely fertile area of attachment theory and research.

Different object relations theorists (e.g., Fairbairn, 1952, 1994; Klein, 1955/2002a, 1975/2002b) have different models of internalization. For example, Klein theorized that internal objects emerge out of the interaction of real experiences and unconscious fantasies that are instinctively derived. According to her, people are born with instinctually based passions related to both love and aggression that are linked to unconscious fantasies and images about relationships with others. The unconscious fantasies linked to these instincts exist prior to any actual encounter with other human beings and serve as the scaffolding for the perception of others.

In Klein's thinking, instinctually based aggression plays a particularly important role. She believed that infants experience their own aggression as intolerable. For this reason, they need to fantasize that this aggression originates in the other (typically the mother in Klein's thinking) rather than in themselves. Klein uses the term *projective identification* to designate the intrapsychic process through which feelings originating internally are experienced as originating from the other. These unconscious fantasies of aggressive, persecuting others (referred to as *internal objects* by Klein) become part of the infant's psychic world. These aggressive "bad" internal objects then color their perception of significant others who they see as dangerous and persecuting. To retain some perception of the other as potentially good and not persecutory, infants unconsciously split the image of the other or the internal object into good and bad aspects. The good aspect is thus able to remain uncontaminated by the bad aspect. Over time, as a result of both cognitive and emotional maturation and ongoing encounters with real significant others, the child is able to begin integrating the good and bad objects into one whole and to re-own aggression as emerging from the self.

Fairbairn theorized that internal objects are established when the individual withdraws from external reality because the caregiver is unavailable, frustrating, or traumatizing, and instead creates a type of internal reality as a substitute. According to Fairbairn, to the extent that one has unsatisfying relationships with actual significant others, one becomes preoccupied with fantasized relationships, which become represented unconsciously. These fantasized relationships become important building blocks for one's experience of the self because the self is always experienced in relation to others, whether in fantasy or reality. From Fairbairn's perspective, the problem is that defensive attempts to control significant others by developing fantasized relationships with them, rather than real ones, are ultimately only partially successful. The reason for this is that the depriving or traumatizing aspects of the significant other that provide the raw material for the unconscious fantasy or internal object inevitably end up becoming part of the internal structure or enduring psychic organization that is developed.

## The Movement Toward Psychoanalytic Pluralism in North America

Unlike the British analytic establishment, which formally institutionalized three psychoanalytic traditions, in the United States of the mid-20th century only one psychoanalytic tradition was accepted: ego psychology. American psychoanalysts were by and large unfamiliar with British object relations theory, and American theorists diverging too far from mainstream ego psychology either resigned from or were forced out of the American Psychoanalytic Association and started their own schools of thought.

One of the most notable mavericks was Harry Stack Sullivan (1892–1949), an iconoclastic American-born psychiatrist who had never received any formal psychoanalytic training. Sullivan (e.g., 1953) developed his own model of psychoanalytically oriented psychiatry, which was strongly influenced by a type of social field theory emerging out of the Chicago School of Sociology and symbolic interactionist thinking. Unlike Freud, Sullivan theorized that the need for human relatedness is the most fundamental human motivation, as opposed to instinctual drives. He also believed that it is impossible to understand the individual out of context of relationships with others and that this principle extends to the therapeutic relationship. In contrast to mainstream psychoanalysts, Sullivan argued that everything transpiring in the therapeutic relationship needs to be understood in terms of both the client's and the therapist's ongoing contributions rather than exclusively in terms of the client's psychology or the transference. Although Sullivan published very little (most of his books consist of posthumously published lectures), he had a formative influence on the training of American psychoanalysts, primarily through his lectures and supervising.

Sullivan befriended and became a mentor to another American-born psychiatrist, Clara Thompson (1957). With Sullivan's encouragement, Thompson went to Europe to seek training with Sandor Ferenczi, who was transitioning toward a more interpersonal perspective in his more mature work. Sullivan and Thompson ultimately formed an alliance with Erich Fromm. Fromm, a European-born and European-trained psychoanalyst with a background as a sociologist, had an interest in the synthesis of psychoanalysis and sociological and political thinking. In addition, over time he came to incorporate humanistic and existential ideas into his thinking (e.g., Fromm, 1941). Fromm's perspective placed considerable emphasis on the importance of the authentic human encounter in the therapeutic relationship. In 1946, Sullivan, Thompson, and Fromm founded the William Alanson White Institute in New York. The White

Institute subsequently was the foremost center of American interpersonal psychoanalysis.

Another important figure who came to play a key role in the movement toward a more pluralistic perspective in North American psychoanalysis was Heinz Kohut (1984). Kohut was a European émigré who completed his medical training in Vienna in 1939 and then immigrated to Chicago, where he completed both his residency in psychiatry and his formal psychoanalytic training. For years, Kohut was a well-respected mainstream ego psychologist. As his thinking and clinical work evolved, however, he became particularly interested in the treatment of narcissism, and over time his theoretical formulations diverged increasingly from mainstream psychoanalytic ideas. Kohut aimed to understand the processes through which the individual develops a cohesive sense of the self, an experience of inner vitality, and a capacity for self-esteem. He placed an increasing emphasis on the role that the therapist's empathic stance plays as a mechanism of change in and of itself, and in the centrality of this process in repairing ruptures in the therapeutic relationship when they occur as a result of the therapist's inevitable lapses in empathy.

Rather than focusing on developing adaptive compromise formations, Kohut focused on helping clients to develop a cohesive sense of self and a sense of inner vitality and engagement in meaningful life projects. This emphasis on transforming an inner sense of emptiness into one of vitality and authenticity mirrored important developments taking place in the work of important British Middle Group theorists such as Michael Balint and Donald Winnicott. Ultimately Kohut broke away from the mainstream and founded the tradition of *self psychology*.

The development of relational psychoanalysis was the most important stage in the ultimate fragmentation of the monolithic psychoanalytic perspective that had dominated American psychoanalysis. This was achieved by bringing together a range of psychoanalytic perspectives into a new paradigm. A key publication was Jay Greenberg and Stephen Mitchell's (1983) book *Object Relations in Psychoanalytic Theory*. This book provides a scholarly examination and critique of the work of a broad range of different psychoanalytic theorists from both the United States and Britain. It provides a framework for schematizing the relationship between various key psychoanalytic theorists and for understanding both the intellectual and sociopolitical factors leading to the evolution of their approaches. Greenberg and Mitchell argued that the entire history of psychoanalysis can be understood as the attempt to develop an interpersonal model of motivation and functioning without discarding Freud's model of motivation, which is based on drive theory.

Greenberg and Mitchell's (1983) book accomplished numerous objectives. First, it established a legitimate role for the tradition of American interpersonal psychoanalysis within the mainstream psychoanalytic tradition by drawing parallels between what Sullivan was trying to accomplish theoretically and what more mainstream psychoanalysts were attempting to achieve (e.g., Heinz Hartmann, Edith Jacobson, Margaret Mahler, Otto Kernberg). They illustrated the way in which a range of different theorists, including Sullivan, were attempting to elaborate on the interpersonal aspects of psychoanalysis that were implicit in Freud's thinking but not conceptualized in a theoretically systematic and coherent fashion. They introduced Sullivan's interpersonal perspective to an audience of ego psychologists who were by and large unfamiliar with it. Just as important, they introduced both interpersonal analysts and American ego psychologists to the seminal work of British object relations theorists such as Klein, Fairbairn, and Winnicott.

Subsequent decades have seen many important developments in theory and practice within a relational framework, which are spelled out in the subsequent chapters of this book. Of particular note is the work of analysts, including Phillip Bromberg, who proposed a model of the mind as consisting of multiple self-states that may be in conflict with one another and that emerge in different relational contexts (e.g., Bromberg, 1998, 2006; Harris, 2008; Mitchell, 1993; Pizer, 1998). The concepts of affect regulation and mentalization, coming out of attachment theory, have been increasingly influential on relational thinkers (Fonagy, Gergely, Jurist, & Target, 2002). In addition, the work of Lew Aron (1996, 2006) on mutuality in the therapeutic relationship and the work of Jessica Benjamin (1988, 2018) on intersubjectivity have been significant historical developments in our understanding of the mind and how to work with it in treatment.

## Klein and Post-Kleinian Traditions in Europe and Latin America

Because this book is aimed primarily at an American audience, the focus has been on developments that have had the greatest influence on the American psychoanalytic tradition. At the same time, two additional developments have been influential in other parts of the world and are now having an impact on American psychoanalysis. The first development can be designated as Kleinian and post-Kleinian thinking. A host of innovative thinkers in various parts of Europe and Latin America have built on Kleinian thinking in creative and clinically useful ways. Of particular note is the Kleinian or neo-Kleinian emphasis on careful moment-by-moment monitoring of the extent to which the client is making constructive use of the therapist's interventions, as well as the potential role that the client's feelings of badness and inadequacy and envy of the therapist's apparent goodness and bountifulness can play in his or her inability to make constructive use of therapeutic interventions (e.g., Joseph, 1989). Examples of extremely influential Kleinian and post-Kleinian theorists in Latin America and continental Europe include Heinrich Racker, Willi and Madeline Baranger, Leon Grinberg, Horacio Etchegoyen, Ignacio Matte-Blanco, and Antonino Ferro (Etchegoyen, 1991; Ferro, 2002). Many of these theorists have also been profoundly influenced by the prominent neo-Kleinian analyst Wilfred Bion (1970).

## Lacanian Theory

A final major psychoanalytic tradition is Lacanian and post-Lacanian theory. This tradition, which originated in the work of French psychoanalyst Jacques Lacan (1901–1981), played a central role in the development of French psychoanalysis. It has also become highly influential in Latin America (especially Argentina) and has had an important influence on psychoanalysis in continental Europe and increasingly in England. In the United States, the influence of Lacanian thought has mostly been limited to the areas of literary criticism, the humanities, and feminist thinking. But Lacanian concepts are beginning to make their way into American clinical psychoanalysis as well. Lacan is notoriously difficult to understand, in part because his thinking is embedded in the context of the French intellectual tradition that is stylistically very different from the Anglo-American intellectual tradition.

Lacan (1975/1988a, 1978/1988b) was extremely critical of the American tradition of ego psychology, which he viewed as betraying Freud's most radical and important insights about the centrality of unconscious processes and of emphasizing conventionality and adaptation to society. In contrast to American ego psychologists who emphasized the adaptive aspects of the ego, Lacan argued that the ego (i.e., one's sense of "I") is an illusion. According to Lacan, our identity or sense of "I-ness" is forged out of a misidentification of ourselves with the desire of the other. This begins in our childhood when we attempt to satisfy the desire of others, initially as incarnated in the desires of the mother; in other terms, one could say that we develop a sense of who we are through the construction of an identity that is designed to satisfy the needs and fantasies of our parents. Unlike Winnicott (or for that matter, humanistic psychotherapists), however, Lacan does not believe that there is a true self waiting to be discovered, underlying the illusory sense of "I" that we experience. Instead, there is emptiness, or what Lacan refers to as a *lack*—a fundamental sense of alienation from the self. This fundamental experience of alienation or lack stems from a variety of sources. One of the most important is that our experience cannot be symbolized or communicated without the medium of language. The very process of symbolizing our experience through language, however, results in a distortion of this experience and contributes to the experience of alienation.

If there is no true self waiting to be discovered or uncovered, what is the essence of cure from a Lacanian perspective? Lacanian theory is ambiguous on this point. On one hand, Lacan emphasized the importance of developing a true ownership of one's own desire and a separation from the desire of the other. On the other hand, he argued that desire by its very nature can never be satisfied. There is thus a level at which Lacan appears to be saying that an important goal of analysis is to accept this intrinsic lack and to come to terms with it (Moncayo, 2008).

Lacan developed an iconic status in French culture because of his radical challenge to conventional rules and his attacks on traditional societal standards. Furthermore, Lacan strongly promoted accepting candidates from a wide range of educational backgrounds into psychoanalytic training and challenged existing psychoanalytic orthodoxies and forms of authoritarianism. His intellectual engagement with well-known French left-wing intellectuals also contributed to his popularity. Psychoanalysis in France blossomed and emerged as a progressive and revolutionary force at precisely the same time as psychoanalysis in the United States was becoming a more conservative cultural institution.

In Latin America, Lacanian psychoanalysis emerged as an important cultural force in the climate of political ferment leading up to the emergence of the dictatorships of the 1970s and 1980s. Unlike France, countries such as Argentina and Brazil had well-established psychoanalytic establishments by this time. The dominant psychoanalytic associations were beginning to splinter into conservative apolitical factions, and a younger generation of analysts felt that an apolitical or accommodationist stance in the face of oppressive totalitarian regimes was indefensible. The anti-authoritarian, politically subversive elements of the Lacanian tradition, as well as its connection to left-wing intellectual circles, played important roles in enhancing its appeal. With the downfall of the various dictatorships in Latin America in the early to mid-1980s, Lacan's influence blossomed more fully (Plotkin, 2001).

# 3

# Theory

What are the values and goals of psychoanalysis and psychoanalytically oriented theory and therapy? There is no simple
answer to this question given the host of different psychoanalytic traditions and the evolving nature of psychoanalysis. Nevertheless, I attempt
to articulate a few of the key values represented within a range of diverse
psychoanalytic traditions, some of them complementary and some existing
in tension with one another.

## PSYCHOANALYSIS AS A BOUNDARY DISCIPLINE

Psychoanalysis has been classified alternatively as a medical discipline,
a science, an interpretive or hermeneutic system, a philosophical system,
and a form of cultural criticism. Whereas Freud was intent on establishing
psychoanalysis as a science, many contemporary critics have argued that

http://dx.doi.org/10.1037/0000190-003
*Psychoanalysis and Psychoanalytic Therapies, Second Edition*, by J. D. Safran and J. Hunter

it is a "failed science" (e.g., Grunbaum, 1984). At the same time, there is a tendency among many contemporary proponents of psychoanalysis to argue that the attempt to think of psychoanalysis as science was misguided in the first place and that psychoanalysis is more accurately conceptualized as a hermeneutic or an interpretive discipline. Although many psychoanalytic concepts have not been tested empirically, and many are unverifiable to begin with, a host of empirical studies support a range of different psychoanalytic concepts (for a review of some of this empirical literature, see Westen, 1998; Westen & Gabbard, 1999). A substantial and growing body of research also supports the effectiveness of psychoanalytic treatment (Leichsenring, Leweke, Klein, & Steinert, 2015; Levy, Ablon, & Kaechele, 2012; Shedler, 2010).

Notwithstanding this growing evidence, debates such as whether it is best to conceptualize psychoanalysis as a science or a hermeneutic discipline will inevitably continue, I believe, because psychoanalysis lies on the boundary between various intellectual and scientific disciplines. This liminal status has led to considerable confusion about how to think about psychoanalysis, but it has also been an important source of vitality.

## PSYCHOANALYSIS AND THE NATURE OF MENTAL HEALTH

To begin thinking about the goals of psychotherapy, it is essential to make some assumptions about what psychological health looks like. Different forms of psychotherapy and different psychoanalytic traditions hold different assumptions about what a good life is, which affects the goals of treatment. Freud's (1895/1955) oft-quoted remark that psychoanalysis transforms neurotic misery into ordinary unhappiness is seen by some as reflecting a pessimistic perspective on life. But it can also be seen as embodying a certain form of wisdom. Freud believed that life by its very nature involves various forms of suffering: illness, loss of loved ones and friends, disappointments, and ultimately death. It is essential, however, to distinguish what might be termed *existential suffering* from self-imposed neurotic suffering. From Freud's perspective, one of the goals of psychoanalysis is to help people learn to grapple with life's inevitabilities with a certain degree of equanimity and dignity.

Many contemporary psychoanalysts have emphasized the goal of living life with vitality. Dimen (2010), paraphrasing author Andrew Solomon, said that "good treatment restores vitality, not happiness" (p. 264). In addition, for many contemporary psychoanalysts there is an emphasis on challenging potentially oppressive normative emphases on singular and conventional definitions of "mental health" and on replacing them with a respect for and appreciation of the infinite number of ways of being in this world and a celebration of this diversity. In the words of influential British psychoanalyst Donald Winnicott (1958), "We are poor indeed if we are only sane" (p. 150).

In numerous respects psychoanalysis goes against the grain of many values that are characteristic of our culture and that are reflected in such developments as the managed care system and the evidence-based treatment movement. The managed care system, the evidence-based treatment models, and the dominance of cognitive–behavioral tradition promote such values as clarity, activity, speed, concreteness, practicality, realism, efficiency, systematization, and consistency and limit goals to the absence of diagnosable symptoms.

Psychoanalysis, in contrast, tends to value such dimensions as complexity, depth, nuance, and patience and aims to address character issues that keep the patient from living fully. These values can be traced back to some aspects of Freud's early thinking and are expressed in different ways in different psychoanalytic traditions. Freud cautioned analysts that the "furor sanandi" (an excessive zeal to cure) could interfere with the therapist's ability to assume the kind of attitude of patience and acceptance that is necessary to be truly helpful. Wilfred Bion (1970) is famous for speaking about the importance of approaching every session "without memory or desire" in order to allow the "emotional truth" of what is taking place to emerge (p. 57).

The downside of this type of perspective is that it can lend itself to the type of never-ending analysis that is caricatured in Woody Allen movies and that clients have valid reasons to be concerned about. In fact, some very prominent analysts have argued that this attitude can too often degenerate into a failure to grapple with the question of what is genuinely helpful to clients and is one of the factors that has led to the declining popularity of psychoanalysis (Renik, 2006). On the other hand, this emphasis can serve as a valuable corrective to the contemporary Western tendency to overestimate our capacity for individual efficacy and mastery and that fails to recognize the limitation of our ability to "have it all."

## Complexity, Ambiguity, and Curiosity

Psychoanalysis tends toward the view that at a fundamental level, human beings are complex creatures whose experience and actions are shaped by multiple and often conflicting conscious and unconscious determinants, as well as by social and cultural forces. Related to this is an emphasis on the importance of tolerance of ambiguity. Psychoanalytic thinking assumes that given the complexity of human experience, there is a fundamental ambiguity to the therapeutic process. This sense of ambiguity forecloses the possibility of pat understandings of what is going on with one's client or in the therapeutic process. This can lead to a fair amount of anxiety for novice therapists who want to feel that they can understand what is going on in a definitive fashion and have clear guidelines for practice. The positive side of this fundamental ambiguity is that it encourages genuine curiosity for watching the process emerge and allowing one's understanding to unfold and evolve over time (McWilliams, 2004). This is associated with a genuine respect for the complexity of human nature and a feeling of humility in the face of the ultimate unknowability of things.

## The Ethic of Honesty

Freud believed in the importance of shedding one's illusions and coming to accept the inevitabilities of life. He believed that self-deception is ubiquitous, and he valued the process of self-reflection and truth seek-ing (in the sense of searching for one's real motives). One could say that psychoanalysis is associated with an ethic of honesty (McWilliams, 2004; M. G. Thompson, 2004). Clients are encouraged to strive to be truthful with themselves about their own motives, and this type of honesty is expected of therapists as well.

Once we accept the idea of unconscious motivation, we recognize that we are all, at some level, strangers to ourselves. We begin to see that we therapists are just as susceptible to self-deception as our clients are. It is not unusual for trainees in supervision to figure out that they were intervening in a certain way because of feelings they were completely unaware of (e.g., competitiveness, insecurity, irritation, a desire for control) and that our rational or theoretical understanding of why we are acting as we are as therapists is often only part of the story or an after-the-fact justification.

Conducting psychotherapy from a psychoanalytic perspective thus inevitably involves an ongoing process of self-discovery and personal growth for therapists. It is difficult to work with clients, especially chal-lenging ones, without being willing to explore one's own contribution to what is going on in the therapeutic relationship in an ongoing fashion and a willingness to reflect on why we are doing what we are doing in a given session. Many contemporary psychoanalysts believe that in many successful treatments, both the client and the therapist change as they learn about themselves.

## A Search for Meaning, Vitality, and Authenticity

Freud's emphasis was on becoming aware of our irrational, instinctually based wishes and then renouncing or taming them through our rational faculties. One change in the goals of contemporary psychoanalytic thinking is an increased focus on creating meaning and revitalizing the self. This shift in clinical sensibility corresponds to changes in the cultural landscape from Freud's time to ours. Psychoanalysis was born during an era when individualism was in the process of becoming more pronounced. In the Victorian culture of Freud's time, the self was viewed as dangerous, and an emphasis was placed on self-mastery and self-control (Cushman, 1995). Over the last century, the culture of individualism has continued to evolve, and the people have become increasingly isolated from community. This is a double-edged sword. On one hand, the more individuated person of contemporary culture is freer of the potentially suffocating judgment from community. On the other hand, he or she is cut off from the sense of meaning and well-being that potentially flows from integration with a wider community.

The disintegration of the unifying web of beliefs and values that traditionally held people together has resulted in the emergence of what Philip Cushman (1995) referred to as the *empty self*. This empty self experiences the lack of tradition, community, and shared meaning as an internal hollowness; a lack of personal conviction and worth; and a chronic, undifferentiated emotional hunger. In contemporary Western culture, psychological conflicts are thus more likely to involve a search for authentic meaning and a hunger for intimate and meaningful rela-tionships than a conflict between sexual instincts and cultural norms (Mitchell, 1993; Safran, 2017).

Philosophers and historians tell us that the concept of authenticity is a relatively novel invention that emerged in 18th-century Europe (Guignon, 2004; Taylor, 1992). Its emergence was associated with the rise of the culture of Romanticism. The Romantic movement can be under-stood as a backlash against the Enlightenment, an attempt to recover a sense of oneness and wholeness lost with the rise of modernity. The Romantic movement holds that truth is discovered not through scientific investigation or by logic but through immersion in one's deepest feelings. There is a distrust of society in the Romantic movement and an implicit belief in the existence of an inner "true self" that is in harmony with nature. Conventional social rituals are seen as artificial and empty and as potentially stifling authenticity. Consistent with this sensibility, there is an important thread in contemporary psychoanalytic thinking that views the therapist's authentic responsiveness to the client as a significant element in the change process. The therapist's ability to act spontaneously or to improvise in response to the demands of the moment is viewed as a potential antidote to the devitalizing effects of social ritual and conformity in people's lives (Ringstrom, 2007; D. N. Stern et al., 1998). Irwin Hoffman has persuasively argued that it is important not to emphasize the value of spontaneity at the expense of ritual, and vice versa. He has argued instead for the value of thinking in terms of the dialectical interplay between ritual and spontaneity in the therapeutic process; the interested reader is referred to I. Z. Hoffman (1998).

## Reflection-in-Action Versus Technical Rationality

At a time when there is a growing emphasis in the psychotherapy field on the importance of developing evidence-based practices that can be delivered in a standardized fashion, there is a contrasting trend in contemporary psychoanalytic thinking to emphasize the unique nature of every therapeutic encounter and the impossibility of developing "standardized" interventions or principles of intervention. The idea that professional knowledge consists of "instrumental problem solving made rigorous by the application of scientific theory and technique" is referred to as *technical rationality* by Schön (1983, p. 21). Of interest, Schön and others conducting research on differences in the problem-solving styles of experts versus novices (e.g., Dreyfus & Dreyfus, 1986) have found that skilled practitioners across a wide range of disciplines (musicians, architects, engineers, managers, psychotherapists) do not problem solve in a manner consistent with this model of technical rationality. Instead, they engage in a process of what Schön termed *reflection-in-action*. This entails an ongoing appraisal of the evolving situation in a rapid, holistic, and (at least partially) tacit fashion. The process involves a reflective conversation with the relevant situation that allows for modification of one's understanding and actions in response to ongoing feedback.

Contemporary psychoanalytic thinkers have argued that this notion of reflection-in-action provides a better framework for conceptualizing the therapeutic activities of a skilled therapist than does the model of technical rationality (Aron, 1999; I. Z. Hoffman, 2009; Safran & Muran, 2000).

The therapist can no longer look toward a unitary and universal set of principles to guide their actions. Instead, therapists are confronted with a multiplicity of theoretical perspectives that they can use to help them reflect on how best to act in this particular moment with this particular client. Any guidelines derived from theory must ultimately be integrated with a therapist's own irreducible subjectivity (Renik, 1993) and with the unique subjectivity of the client to find a way of being that is facilitative in a given moment.

# KEY CONCEPTS

In this section, I outline some of the central concepts of psychoanalytic thinking. Most, if not all, of these concepts have evolved over time. In addition, whereas some of these concepts originated in the early days of psychoanalytic thinking, others emerged at later stages in the evolution of psychoanalytic theory.

## The Unconscious

The concept of the unconscious is central to psychoanalytic theory. Over time, psychoanalytic conceptualizations have evolved, and these days, divergent models of the unconscious are emphasized by different psycho-analytic schools. Freud's original model of the unconscious suggested that certain memories and associated affects are split off from consciousness because they are too threatening to the individual. As Freud's thinking about the unconscious developed, he began to use the term *primary process* for the unconscious level of cognition. In primary process, there is no distinction between past, present, and future. Different feelings and experiences can be condensed together into one image or symbol, feelings can be expressed metaphorically, and the identities of people can be merged. The "language" of primary process does not operate in accordance with the rational, sequential rules of secondary process or consciousness. Primary process can be glimpsed in dreams and fantasy and underlies disowned wishes or feelings. Secondary process is more conscious and is the foundation for rational, reflective thinking. It takes the disorderly unconscious and makes it logical and sequential.

Freud came to think of the unconscious not only in terms of traumatic memories that had been split off but also in terms of instinctual impulses and associated wishes that are not allowed into awareness because they are unacceptable through cultural conditioning. These instincts and associated wishes are often related to the areas of sexuality and aggression. For example, a woman has sexual feelings toward her sister's husband but disavows them or pushes them out of awareness because she experiences them as too threatening. Freud referred to the process through which unacceptable wishes are kept out of awareness as *repression.*

Many contemporary interpersonal and relational psychoanalysts find it more useful to think of the mind as consisting of multiple self-states that to varying degrees may be in conflict with one another and that emerge in different relational contexts (e.g., Bromberg, 1998, 2006; Davies, 1996; Harris, 2008; Mitchell, 1993; Pizer, 1998). From this perspective, there is no central executive control in the form of the ego. Consciousness is a function of a coalition of different self-states. It is thus an emergent product of a self-organizing system that is influenced in an ongoing fashion by current interpersonal context. From a developmental perspective, experience taking place in the context of interpersonal transactions that are intensely anxiety provoking or traumatic can be kept out of awareness. But there is no hypothetical psychic agency keeping it out of awareness. Instead, there is a failure to attend to the experience and construct a narrative about it (D. B. Stern, 1997, 2010). It is therefore this failure of attention and construction that leads to the splitting off or dissociation of aspects of experience. And just as the interpersonal context leads to the dissociation of experience in the first place, we need others to help us attend to and construct a narrative about it. As Donnel Stern (2010) put it, the therapist thus serves as an essential "partner in thought" for the client.

Whether the unconscious is conceptualized in traditional Freudian terms or in terms of aspects of experience that are not symbolized (or self-states that are dissociated), the concept of the unconscious is central to psychoanalytic thinking. For most psychoanalysts, one of Freud's (1920) most important insights is that we are not masters of our own home. We are all motivated by forces outside of our awareness.

## Fantasy

Psychoanalytic theory holds that fantasies play a meaningful role in psychic functioning and the way in which people relate to external experience. Fantasies vary in the extent to which they are part of conscious awareness— ranging from daydreams and fleeting fantasies on the edge of awareness to deeply unconscious fantasies that are defended against. In Freud's early thinking, these fantasies were linked to instinctually derived wishes and served the function of a type of imaginary wish fulfillment. In this view of fantasies, they are typically linked to sexuality or aggression. Over time Freud and other analysts developed a more elaborated view that sees fantasies as serving a number of psychic functions, including regulating self-esteem, offering a feeling of safety, aiding in regulating affect, and helping to master trauma. Because fantasies are viewed as motivating our behavior and shaping our experience, yet for the most part operate outside of focal awareness, exploring and interpreting clients' fantasies are important parts of the psychoanalytic process.

## One-Person Versus Two-Person Psychologies

A significant development that has taken place across a range of different psychoanalytic schools has been a shift from what has come to be termed a *one-person psychology* to a *two-person psychology.* Freud's original view of the therapist as an objective and neutral observer who could serve as a blank screen onto whom the client projects their transference has been replaced with a view of the therapist and client as coparticipants who engage in an ongoing process of mutual influence at both conscious and unconscious levels. The conceptual shift has important implications for the evolution of many of the concepts we discuss (e.g., resistance, transference, countertransference), as well as for psychoanalytic technique, because it implies that the therapist cannot develop an accurate understanding of the client without developing some awareness of the therapist's own ongoing contribution to the interaction. Although the therapist's goal still remains one of ultimately understanding and helping the client, this cannot be accomplished without an ongoing process of self-exploration on the therapist's part. This is especially the case with difficult or more disturbed clients, who tend to evoke complex feelings and reactions in others. But the process of exploring one's own contributions to the therapeutic relationship can help to illuminate subtle aspects of psychic functioning and interpersonal style in less disturbed clients as well.

## Knowledge and Authority

Traditionally psychoanalysis has emphasized the therapist's ability to know things about clients that they cannot see themselves. This is both because we are all inevitably blinded by our own limits to conscious awareness and because therapists have an advantage with respect to understanding things as a result of their training, expertise, and own personal growth. Privileging the therapist's understanding has exacerbated a power imbalance within the therapeutic relationship and can lead to abuses of the therapist's authority. This disparity could make a client feel that they are being denigrated or patronized. Because the client is the one seeking help from the therapist, he or she is inevitably less empowered.

In Freud's time, it was assumed that therapists had a type of objectivity that clients did not have and that because of clients' unconscious conflict and inability to break through their own defenses and become aware of unconscious experience, therapists both by virtue of their specialized training and personal analysis and their ability to see clients from the outside had the ability to interpret clients' unconscious conflicts. As discussed earlier, in contemporary psychoanalytic thinking there has been a shift toward a two-person psychology and a greater focus on the mutuality of the therapeutic relationship. The therapist is no longer seen as the expert on the client's unconscious. Moreover, with the growing emphasis on the therapist's inevitable embeddedness in the interpersonal field and increased transparency, there is more of a sense that reality is "up for grabs" in the therapeutic relationship.

## Defenses

One of an analyst's most important tools for understanding a client is their pattern of defensive functioning. A defense is an intrapsychic process that works to avoid psychic pain by pushing thoughts, wishes, feelings, or fantasies out of awareness. In traditional psychoanalysis, defenses were viewed as a way to keep sexual or aggressive impulses out of awareness, but a more current view sees defenses as serving many purposes, including maintaining self-esteem, keeping a sense of connection to others, and dealing with threatening feelings ranging from anxiety to terror. Defenses are necessary to deal with everyday life and are often adaptive. We could not function if we experienced all of our thoughts and feelings all of the time, and we need to diffuse reactions with techniques such as humor. However, when defenses are rigid and/or out of awareness, they can be highly problematic and correlate with pathology. For example, if a person defends against fear of abandonment by angrily finding fault with the other, it would be difficult to sustain closeness.

In the heyday of ego psychology, a systematic attempt was made to conceptualize and categorize defenses. A distinction was made between higher level defenses and lower level defenses. The higher level or mature defenses are associated with neurotic functioning; examples include intellectualization, where using abstract ideas keeps the feelings distanced, and undoing, where an impulse that is felt to be unacceptable is transformed into its opposite. Disowned anger toward a friend might lead to flattery, for example. Lower level defenses are also called *primitive* and are associated with character disorders and psychotic symptomatology. Three examples are denial, where objective reality is not acknowledged; dissociation, where consciousness is disrupted in an effort to deal with an upsetting reality; and projection, where internal feelings and impulses are seen as being outside the self. An example of dissociation and denial could be feeling spaced out and "forgetting" that someone has died.

The pattern of defenses that a person relies on can also be associated with character. It can be helpful to think about how a given person deals with anxiety and to differentiate, for example, between an obsessive and a hysterical defensive style. Someone who is obsessive will want to get all of the facts, justify difficult feelings, and repeat thoughts over and over again in their head as a way to not be overwhelmed by affect. This pattern has been associated with a variety of higher level defenses such as intellectualization, rationalization, and isolation of affect but could also involve lower level defenses such as denial and schizoid withdrawal. A hysterical personality style will manifest by someone avoiding acknowledging or forgetting what they know to be true and having strong affective reactions as well as a tendency to avoid disturbing affect through actions or somatic experiences. This style is associated with the defenses of repression, acting out, and somatization. People do not generally fall into clear and consistent character types; they rely on a broad range of defenses. Nonetheless, understanding the way they typically defend against painful affect can be an important tool for the analyst and the patient alike. For example, a client may come to understand, with the analyst's help, that when they agree to something that they do not really want to do, they tend to over-justify all the reasons why it is a good idea (rationalization) and then later feel resentful. If they could learn to acknowledge the initial threatening feeling (anger at being put-upon), they might not fall into this dysfunctional repetitive pattern.

An important defense that has not entered the popular lexicon is referred to as *splitting*. Splitting involves keeping different aspects of a person or relationship unintegrated and not reconciling the distinct aspects. It is often seen when an individual attempts to see someone as all good, uncontaminated by negative feelings they have about them until such time as the script flips and the person becomes all bad. Melanie Klein believed that children normally have difficulty developing a complex representation of the mother that includes both the desirable and undesirable characteristics, so they establish two separate representations: one that is all good and one that is all bad. Klein saw the ability to integrate the two and experience ambivalence as a developmental achievement. Clients who never achieve this ability as adults and rely on the defense of splitting (e.g., borderline clients) will experience dramatic fluctuations in their perception of and feelings toward others. These intense fluctuations make it difficult to maintain stable relationships and difficult to rely on a therapist in a consistent manner.

## Resistance

*Resistance* is conceptualized as the tendency for the individual to try not to change or act in a way that undermines the therapeutic process. Resistance is the way in which defensive processes manifest in the therapy session so as to interfere with the treatment. For example, the client's inability to think of anything to say while in the session may be understood as a form of resistance. The tendency to consistently come late for sessions or to forget about sessions can be thought of as resistance. In both examples, a primary motivating factor may be the unconscious wish to avoid emotional pain (e.g., the pain associated with exploring threatening feelings or the fear of changing). This tendency to avoid pain or fear manifests in a behavior that thwarts or impedes the therapist's agenda and the process of treatment.

There are many potential sources of resistance, including the avoidance of threatening feelings being evoked by the therapeutic process, the equation of change with the experience of self-annihilation, a fear that trusting the therapist will lead to abandonment and more pain, envy of the therapist, or negative feelings toward the therapist that are in part a function of the individual's dynamics.

The concept of resistance, although potentially valuable, can also be problematic. One problem is that the term *resistance* tends to have a connotation of the client doing something wrong, insofar as he or she is not cooperating with the therapist in the therapeutic process. The concept can thus have a blaming or pathologizing quality. Over time, a change in analytic theory and technique has taken place in which resistance has come to be seen not as an obstacle but as an intrinsic part of the client's psychic functioning or aspect of his or her character that needs to be illuminated and understood rather than bypassed. Moreover, greater emphasis has been placed on the self-protective aspects of resistance. There has therefore been an important shift toward conceptualizing the notion of resistance in empathic and affirmative terms. One way of thinking about resistance is to recognize that we have complex and contradictory needs and motivations and that there is a natural tendency to be ambivalent about changing. We begin therapy wanting both to change and to stay the same (Bromberg, 1995). This desire to stay the same (which is typically unconscious) can be grounded in many factors, including a fear of losing our identities and a fear that if we give up our habitual ways of defining ourselves and relating to others, we will experience both complete abandonment and a loss of a sense of self.

Even if resistance is conceptualized in empathic or affirmative terms, there is a natural tendency for therapists to experience resistance as problematic because it obstructs their therapeutic goals and agendas. It is thus not uncommon for therapists to become frustrated or irritated with clients when resistance emerges and to respond in an attempt to break through or interpret away the resistance in order to move on with the work of therapy. It can be helpful to remember that the process of exploring the resistance is the essence of the therapeutic process rather than the work that needs to be done to get to the point at which one can begin therapy.

Another evolution in the conceptualization of resistance reflects the previously mentioned shift from a one-person psychology to a two-person psychology. Whereas a one-person psychology locates the source of the resistance in the client, a two-person psychology emphasizes that the therapist often plays a significant role in the development of resistance. Resistance often emerges in part as a reaction to the therapist's failure of accurate empathic understanding. Resistance can also be a function of more subtle contributions of the therapist to the interaction. For example, a therapist who unconsciously fears dealing with feelings of grief may collude with a client in not fully exploring feelings about the loss of a loved one. A therapist may collude with the client in the process of keeping the conversation at an intellectual level because the theme resonates with painful experiences in the therapist's own life. The exploration or interpretation of resistance often involves an exploration of the therapist's contribution to the resistance (Safran & Muran, 2000).

## Transference

Like most psychoanalytic concepts, the notion of *transference* has evolved considerably since Freud first developed it in 1905. Transference refers to clients' tendency to view the therapist in terms that are shaped by their experiences with important caregivers and other significant figures from their early life. Developmental experiences establish templates or schemas that shape the perception of people in the present. Although this tendency to transfer relational experience happens in many different contexts, the analytic relationship is particularly fertile ground. The caretaking role of the therapist makes him or her a good stand-in for parental figures as issues of nurturance and authority get activated.

The therapeutic relationship thus provides an opportunity for the client to, in a sense, bring the memory of the relationship with the parent or other significant figure from the past (aspects of which are often unconscious) to life through the relationship with the therapist. This provides the therapist with an opportunity to help clients gain insight into how their experiences with significant figures in the past have resulted in unresolved conflicts that influence their current relationships. Because transference entails a type of reliving of clients' early relationships in the present, the therapist's observations and feedback can help them to see their own contributions to the situation in an emotionally alive way. The resulting insight will have an experiential quality to it that will lead to change rather than a purely intellectual understanding that has no ultimate impact on the client.

Early conceptualizations of transference assumed that it involves a distortion of objective reality. It was common to make a distinction between transferential aspects of the therapeutic relationship that are distorted and nontransferential perceptions that are more accurate or reality based. The assumption is that the client's psychological problems make it difficult for him or her to perceive objective reality accurately, and therapists have the ability to provide more objectively based feedback that can correct the client's distorted perceptions. With the growing influence of a two-person psychology, transference has come to be viewed as the joint product of the client's perceptions and the therapist's actual characteristics and actions. This is a critical shift in conceptualization, and its importance cannot be overestimated.

There are two problems with the traditional perspective. First, the assumption that the therapist is the ultimate authority on reality exacerbates the inherent power imbalance in the therapeutic relationship and contributes to the client's feelings of being disempowered and the therapist's potential abuse of this power imbalance. Second, although it is inevitably the case that the client's perceptions of the therapist will be influenced by past experiences, it is problematic to assume that his or her perceptions of the therapist are distorted. What if the client's perception that the therapist is critical or withholding (or shy, sadistic, or flirtatious) has some basis in the therapist's actual characteristics? Or what if certain aspects of the client's behavior elicit reactions on the therapist's part that are consistent with the client's expectations? For example, a client who anticipates that therapist will be abusive in the same way as his or her father or mother had been may act in a hostile way toward the therapist, thereby eliciting hostile or abusive behavior from the therapist. The client's perception of the therapist as abusive is thus not a distortion. It is the client's construction of the current situation influenced by a combination of factors, and treating it as a distortion could be damaging to the client.

## Countertransference

*Countertransference* is the analyst's counterpart to the client's transference. Freud conceptualized countertransference as the therapist's feelings and reactions to the client's transference that are a function of his or her own unresolved unconscious conflicts. For example, a male therapist whose mother tended to play the role of the martyr may have extremely strong negative reactions to a client who takes a similar stance. From Freud's perspective, countertransference reactions were an obstacle to therapy, and the therapist's task was to analyze or work through his or her own countertransference in personal supervision, in therapy, or through self-analysis.

These days, countertransference tends to be defined more broadly as the totality of the therapist's reactions to the client (including feelings, associations, fantasies, and fleeting images). In the same way that a two-person psychology makes it impossible to view transference exclusively as the client's distortion, it is also incompatible with conceptualizing countertransference as stemming from the therapist's unresolved conflicts. Instead, the analyst's thoughts and feelings toward the client are understood as an inevitable by-product of the relational matrix. Countertransference is viewed as providing the therapist with potentially valuable information about the client. Treating therapist experience as clinical information can go too far: Some psychoanalysts assume that their countertransference provides an infallible source of information about the client's unconscious experience and underemphasize the therapist's unique contribution to the countertransference.

Different theorists emphasize different ways of making use of countertransference. On one end of the spectrum, some analysts recommend selectively disclosing certain aspects of their subjective experience with the client as a way of deepening the exploratory process. Certain therapists go as far as to share their fantasies or dreams that might be relevant to the analytic process. Others are more cautious about the disclosure of the countertransference experience to clients and instead emphasize the value of a type of internal work in which one reflects on one's experience privately and makes use of it to help formulate thoughts about what might be going on between the client and therapist and what implications this might have for understanding the client (e.g., Bollas, 1992; Jacobs, 1991; Ogden, 1994).

## Enactment

*Enactments* are repetitive scenarios played out in the relationship between client and therapist that reflect the unconscious contributions of both parties' personal histories, conflicts, and characteristic ways of relating to others. Because client and therapist are always influencing each other at both conscious and unconscious levels, they inevitably end up playing complementary roles in these scenarios. The process of collaborating in the exploration of how each of them is contributing to these scenarios provides clients with an opportunity to see how their own relational schemas contribute to the interaction and to then try to play out new scenarios with other important people in their lives.

The traditional psychoanalytic wisdom was that the therapist should avoid participating in these enactments and instead try to maintain a neutral position from which he or she can interpret the client's transference toward the therapist, thereby helping the client to see how the present is being shaped in maladaptive ways by his or her own unconscious assumptions, projections, and previous developmental experiences.

One problem with aspiring to therapeutic neutrality as an ideal is that it sets up unrealistic standards that lead us to place impossible demands on ourselves, which makes it more difficult to accept and become aware of aspects of our own contribution to the enactment that we experience as shameful or unacceptable. This lack of self-acceptance makes it more likely that we will need to dissociate aspects of our own self-experience, making it harder to ultimately recognize the nature of our participation in the enactment and to dis-embed from it. Furthermore, even if it were possible to avoid participating in enactments with our clients, the ability to do so would deprive us of the experience of participating in our clients' relational worlds and developing a lived experience of what their relational world feels like. The process of participating in these enactments thus allows us, in Philip Bromberg's (1998) words, to know our clients "from outside in." Those things that our clients cannot express to us linguistically are communicated through nonverbal behavior and action, and the only way we can come to know important dissociated aspects of the client's internal experience is to know the feeling of playing a complementary role in their relational scenarios.

A common position in contemporary psychoanalytic thinking, therefore, is that the therapist cannot avoid participating in these enactments no matter how psychologically aware he or she is, because people are inevitably influenced by complex nonverbal communications from others that are difficult to decode and therapists, like other human beings, are never fully transparent to themselves. So the therapeutic challenge is to recognize enactments as they play out and to work them through with patients with a sense of mutual participation.

## The Therapeutic Alliance

The concept of the *therapeutic alliance* originated in early psychoanalytic theory. Although Freud did not use the term explicitly, he did emphasize the importance of establishing a good collaborative relationship with the client. In a seminal article, Richard Sterba (1934) established the groundwork for subsequent thinking about the alliance by arguing that therapy involves a process of developing the capacity for self-observation by identifying with the therapist's observing function.

Perhaps the best-known psychoanalytic formulation of the alliance was articulated by Ralph Greenson in the United States. Greenson (1965) spoke about the importance of distinguishing between the transferential aspects of the therapeutic relationship, which are distorted, and the alliance, which is based on the client's rational, undistorted perception of the therapist and on a feeling of genuine linking, trust, and respect. Greenson emphasized that the caring, human aspects of the therapeutic relationship play a critical role in allowing the client to benefit from the interventions of psychoanalysis.

Many contemporary psychotherapy researchers have found Edward Bordin's (1979) transtheoretical conceptualization of the alliance to be particularly useful. Bordin conceptualized the alliance as consisting of three interdependent components: tasks, goals, and bond. According to him, the strength of the alliance is dependent on the degree of agreement between client and therapist about the tasks and goals of therapy and on the quality of the relational bond between them. The *tasks* of therapy consist of the specific activities (either overt or covert) that the client must engage in to benefit from treatment (e.g., exploring dreams, exploring the transference). The *goals* of therapy are general objectives toward which the treatment is directed (e.g., symptom reduction, personality change). The *bond* element of the alliance refers to the degree of trust that the client has in the therapist and the extent to which he feels understood by the therapist. The bond, task, and goal components of the alliance are always influencing one another. So, for example, to the extent that there is an agreement between client and therapist about tasks and goals, the bond will be strengthened. To the extent that the therapeutic tasks or goals do not initially make sense to the client, a strong bond will make it easier to develop some agreement or working consensus.

Building on Bordin's (1979) thinking, as well as developments in relational psychoanalysis, I, together with my colleagues, have argued that it is more useful to think of the alliance as an ongoing process of negotiation between client and therapist about therapeutic tasks and goals because this emphasizes the importance of mutual attempts by both client and therapist to find ways of working together, rather than placing the burden of responsibility on the client to accommodate to the therapist's way of working (e.g., Safran & Muran, 2000). This ongoing process of negotiation, which is only partially explicit, is an important element of the change process in and of itself. It can provide clients with the opportunity to learn that it is possible to negotiate one's needs with the needs of the other, rather than dealing with conflicts by either denying one's own needs or adopting a rigid stance toward relationships. The ongoing negotiation of the alliance in therapy helps the client to learn that healthy relationships do not have to involve a denial of the other's subjectivity, on one hand, and/or an experience of self-effacement or compromise of one's sense of integrity, on the other.

## The Therapist's Stance

Classical psychoanalytic thinking prescribed clear guidelines for the therapist's stance, which are contained within the principles of abstinence, anonymity, and neutrality. *Abstinence* refers to the therapist's refraining from gratifying clients' wishes and requests when their fulfillment is seen as interfering with the therapeutic process. Early psychoanalytic thinking was influenced by the experience of working with hysterical clients who had a tendency to develop erotic transferences, and Freud advised therapists not to gratify erotic wishes but rather to help clients to understand what was underlying them.

*Anonymity* refers to the therapist not sharing personal information and trying to be a blank slate to receive the patient's projections. *Neutrality* refers to respect for the client's autonomy and attempting to remain objective and not influence the client's decisions. The principle of neutrality reflects the value of psychoanalysis to cure through truth seeking and the uncovering of the unconscious rather than through suggestion.

Although these guidelines still exert some influence on today's psychoanalytic thinking, their implementation has been modified if not completely abandoned by a number of theorists. For example, with respect to the principle of abstinence, although it may be countertherapeutic to agree to a borderline client's request to meet for coffee, it can be therapeutic to speak to a client by phone between sessions. It all depends on the client's unique needs and the specific context.

With respect to the principle of anonymity, the shift toward a two-person psychology and the recognition that the therapist is always conveying information about himself or herself even if attempting to remain anonymous (e.g., through nonverbal behavior, through the type of interventions he or she makes, through decisions about when to remain silent and when to speak) has decreased the emphasis on neutrality as an essential element of the therapist's stance. Nevertheless, contemporary psychoanalytic therapists attempt to retain an ongoing disciplined reflectiveness about the potential impact of disclosing various types of information to the client.

I ask myself, Will answering my client's request for information about my background, my personal life, or my current feelings about the client facilitate or hinder the therapeutic process? Why is my client asking this particular question now? What emotional impact does my client's question have on me? Two clients may ask the identical question (e.g., how many children I have), and I feel perfectly comfortable answering the first client, whereas with the second client I feel it would be more helpful to understand what is behind the query.

## Self-Disclosure

As psychoanalytic thinking about the topic of therapist neutrality has evolved, so too has thinking about the attitude toward self-disclosure. In classical psychoanalysis, it was believed that analysts should say as little about themselves as possible in order not to "contaminate" the transference. The idea was that it would be easier to see patients' distortions and the repetition they represented if they were reacting to a blank screen. At times this led to extreme positions such as a reluctance to answer any questions about details of the therapist's life outside the therapy session (e.g., questions about whether the therapist has ever struggled with issues similar to the client's, or where the therapist is going for a vacation) or the therapist's thoughts or feelings during the session.

Although this perspective on self-disclosure has the advantage of offering unambiguous guidelines and can be facilitative in certain contexts, it has the downside of limiting the therapist's flexibility and in some cases being unnecessarily off-putting and alienating to the client. Under some circumstances, it can be extremely facilitative for the therapist to self-disclose. The therapist's willingness to answer an innocuous question may reduce a sense of artificial distance or formality and facilitate the development of the alliance. In other cases, therapist self-disclosure can interfere with the therapeutic process or have unintended and potentially harmful consequences. As clients, we have ambivalent and conflicting needs about knowing our therapists (Aron, 1996). On one hand, there is the desire for intimacy, the desire to feel close to the therapist, or the desire to reduce the power imbalance by knowing that the therapist is a human being just as we are. On the other hand, we can have the conflicting desire to maintain some aspects of the anonymity of the therapist so that we do not have to worry about the therapist's needs or so that we can maintain the therapist in the role of the helper who has special qualities that will allow him or her to be of assistance to us. In contemporary practice, strict rules about self-disclosure have been replaced with the ubiquitous "it depends." It depends on the type of disclosure, it depends on the unique qualities and needs of the client, and it depends on what is going on in the therapeutic relationship.

Another type of self-disclosure is when the analyst spontaneously shares thoughts or feelings within the session. This form of self-disclosure (often referred to as *countertransference disclosure*) can provide a useful way of providing the client with his or her impact on another human being and may play a vital role in initiating an exploratory process (Ehrenberg, 1992; Safran & Muran, 2000). For example, a therapist who becomes aware of feeling particularly cautious or tentative with a client may, in a curious and inquiring manner, say, "I'm not sure what exactly is going on, but I find myself being very cautious, and tentative with you. . . . It feels almost as if I'm walking on eggshells."

Countertransference disclosures of this type can be a useful way of putting into words something that is taking place implicitly in the therapeutic relationship, thereby holding it up to the light of day, where it can be examined. It is not uncommon in everyday exchanges for people to unconsciously act in ways that subtly impact on others or elicit complex and contradictory reactions that are difficult to understand or put into words. For example, someone may act in a subtly demeaning way toward others that engenders feelings of inadequacy or competitiveness in them. Or someone may habitually have a lively, humorous bantering style that keeps others off-balance and at a distance. The implicit rules of everyday social discourse do not sanction trying to talk about these subtle interactions. As a result, there is a type of ongoing mystification that is perpetuated in relationships, especially for people who are likely to be especially self-defeating. Therapists have the role-conferred permission to break the normal rules of social discourse and to step back and attempt to talk about that which normally goes unexplored.

This tremendously valuable permission provides therapists with a way to facilitate self-awareness in their clients. Like other forms of self-disclosure, however, countertransference disclosure can be either facilitative or hindering, depending on the particular context. For example, a client whose parents were narcissistically self-absorbed may experience the therapist's countertransference disclosure as a form of self-absorption on the therapist's part and as a neglect of the client's needs. A narcissistic client's sense of self may be so fragile that he or she cannot tolerate attending to the subjectivity of the other and may experience the therapist's countertransference disclosure as overwhelming or threatening. It is thus always important for the analyst to be responsive to the needs of the specific client and the unique context when using countertransference disclosure.

## Emotion and Motivation

As previously discussed, for Freud, motivation is based on drives: instinctually derived forces that exist on the boundary between the psychological and the biological. They are a form of psychic energy. In Freud's mature thinking, there are two primary drives: a life instinct and a death instinct. Motivation is conceptualized as a complex interaction between these two drives and also as a product of attempts to reestablish situations that have resulted in satisfaction by facilitating the discharge of psychic energy. There is no systematic model of emotion in Freud's thinking. Freud's drive model was anchored in neurophysiological theory and evolutionary models that were commonly accepted in his time but have since been superseded by other theoretical and empirical developments. Although over the years theorists have made attempts to develop revised or alternative motivational models, one meaningful trend in contemporary psychoanalytic thinking is to replace drive theory with a motivational perspective that is grounded in contemporary developments in emotion theory and research (Safran & Muran, 2000). From this perspective, emotions play a central role in human motivation. Emotions function to safeguard the concerns of the organism. Some of these concerns are biologically programmed, and these correspond to core motivational systems (e.g., Ekman & Davidson, 1994; Frijda, 1986; Greenberg & Safran, 1987; Safran & Greenberg, 1991).

For example, Lichtenberg (1989) theorized that there are five core motivational systems: (a) the need for psychic regulation of physiological requirements, (b) the need for attachment and affiliation, (c) the need for assertion and exploration, (d) the need to react aversively through antagonism or withdrawal, and (e) the need for sensual and sexual pleasure (e.g., attachment, curiosity). Other concerns are a result of learning. Many of these learned concerns are the result of values that result from learning about subgoals that will satisfy the needs of the attachment system. For example, one can learn that one needs to be dependent to maintain a connection with the attachment figure, or others might learn that a type of precocious maturity is important or that sexual desirability plays a role.

## Attachment Theory

John Bowlby believed that Freud's motivational model was inadequate, and he developed an attachment-based model that has become increasingly prominent in mainstream developmental, social and clinical psychology. Bowlby's motivational model combines certain basic psychoanalytic ideas with infant observation research, ethology, and control systems theory (an interdisciplinary branch of engineering and mathematics that deals with the behavior of dynamic systems). Attachment theory has generated a tremendous amount of empirical research in the last few decades and in fact has become one of the most fertile research areas emerging out of psychoanalytic theory. Because articles and books on attachment theory are voluminous (see, e.g., Cassidy & Shaver, 2016, for an excellent review), I risk oversimplifying things by restricting myself here to detailing a few fundamental propositions of attachment theory and exploring the way it fills an important niche in the psychoanalytic perspective on unconscious motivation.

According to Bowlby, humans have an instinctively based need (what attachment theorists refer to as a *motivational system*) to maintain proximity to their primary caregivers (referred to as *attachment figures*; Bowlby, 1969, 1973, 1980). This motivational system, designated the *attachment system,* serves an adaptive function in that it increases the possibility that the infant will be able to obtain the caretaking and protection that are essential for survival. Infants develop internal representations of their interactions that permit them to predict what type of actions will help to maintain proximity to attachment figures and what type of actions will threaten the relationship. Bowlby referred to these representations as *internal working models.* For many years, Bowlby's work was ignored by mainstream psychoanalytic theorists, who regarded his thinking as simplistic and mechanistic. Nevertheless, through the work of a number of empirically minded collaborators studying mother–infant inter-actions, Bowlby's work became increasingly influential within mainstream developmental psychology. Of particular note in this respect is the research of Mary Ainsworth (Ainsworth, Blehar, Waters, & Wall, 1978), who developed the Strange Situation laboratory procedure for observing mother–infant interactions and reliably classifying the attachment status of 1- to 2-year-old infants. This procedure subsequently became the paradigmatic method in attachment research. The ensuing development of the Adult Attachment Interview by Mary Main and her collaborators (e.g., Main, Kaplan, & Cassidy, 1985) has allowed researchers to assess adults' internal working models of attachment through a structured interview and reliable coding system. The development of the Adult Attachment Interview thus became another critical turning point in the evolution of attachment research, and it has given rise to a vast body of empirical research with immensely rich clinical implications (e.g., Steele & Steele, 2008).

The use of the Adult Attachment Interview and the concept of Reflective Functioning (Fonagy, Steele, & Steele, 1991) have given rise to a variety of "mentalization-based treatments" (Bateman & Fonagy, 2016). These treatments address attachment difficulties with the ultimate goal of improving the client's ability to understand and differentiate their own thoughts and those of others. In addition, clinical interventions aimed at promoting secure attachments and preventing child maltreatment have been developed as summarized in the *Handbook of Attachment-Based Interventions* (Steele & Steele, 2018).

# 4

# The Therapy Process

Psychoanalytic therapy is a rich and complex process. In this chapter, I articulate some of the elements of this process and provide case examples illustrating the key aspects of the approach, beginning with the principles of intervention.

## PRINCIPLES OF INTERVENTION

In this section, I discuss the therapy process at the level of principles of intervention. In other words, what are the general principles that guide the psychoanalytic therapist's approach to therapeutic intervention, and what are the specific interventions that he or she uses?

http://dx.doi.org/10.1037/0000190-004
*Psychoanalysis and Psychoanalytic Therapies, Second Edition*, by J. D. Safran and J. Hunter
Copyright © 2020 by the American Psychological Association. All rights reserved.

## Formulation

As discussed in Chapter 3, it can be helpful for analysts to think about their clients in terms of character formulation. In formulating their client's character, a clinician takes into account such factors as the client's characteristic defensive style, ego strengths and weaknesses, capacity for insight, and the nature of his or her internal object relations. Examples of ego strengths include impulse control, judgment, capacity for sustained work, and reality testing.

The topic of case formulation in psychoanalysis is complex, and a vast literature has been devoted to outlining different considerations relevant to it. To begin with, given that there are multiple psychoanalytic theories rather than a uniform psychoanalytic approach, each psycho-analytic theory will lead the therapist to focus on different dimensions, and the same case could be described in a disparate manner. One can formulate a case from the perspective of ego psychology, various models of object relations theory (e.g., Klein, Fairbairn, Winnicott), interpersonal theory, self psychology, Lacanian theory, intersubjectivity theory, or relational psychoanalysis.

Ego psychology or modern conflict theory (the contemporary American version of ego psychology) tends to formulate clinical problems in terms of the internal conflict between unconscious wishes and the defenses against them. For example, an individual might wish to assert himself but feels uncomfortable with this feeling and defends against his wish by being overly accommodating.

Object relations and interpersonal/relational theories tend to formulate cases in terms of internal object relations that lead the individual to play out repetitive internalized patterns. For example, a woman whose father divorced her mother when she was 3 years old and abandoned the family develops an internalized representation of men as emotionally unavailable and a pattern of being attracted to emotionally unavailable romantic partners, in part as a way of recapturing the love of the father who abandoned her.

There is no reason that a clinical formulation cannot synthesize both conflict and relational models. For example, Matthew has an internalized representation of others as intolerant of aggression and has developed a pattern of defending against his aggressive impulses and acting in an overly accommodating way. This relational pattern leads others to take advantage of him, which incurs resentment, which in turn has to be disowned. Although Matthew is not aware of angry feelings, he nevertheless expresses them in a passive-aggressive fashion. This evokes aggressive responses from others, which he feels are unwarranted. This further intensified Matthew's feelings of being an impotent victim.

The process of formulation from a contemporary perspective involves combining information from a number of different sources. The therapist looks for recurrent themes that occur in the stories that clients tell about their current relationships and their past relationships (including their relationships with their parents). The therapist also pays attention to patterns or themes that are beginning to emerge in the therapeutic relationship. This process requires therapists to attend to subtle fluctuations in their own ongoing feelings and experiences and to engage in an ongoing reflection of the nature of their own participation in the relationship.

Although there are multiple theoretical perspectives to guide case formulation from a psychoanalytic perspective and many dimensions that are considered relevant to arriving at an adequate formulation, there is also a long-standing tradition within psychoanalysis of the importance of not letting one's formulations bias or interfere with one's ability to be open to emergent information. In early technical papers Freud wrote about the importance of the therapist learning to cultivate an attitude of evenly hovering attention so that the therapist is able to hear and see things that are not necessarily consistent with his or her expectations (Freud, 1912/1958). But there is a tension even within Freud's writing between his emphasis on the importance of the therapist cultivating a tolerance of uncertainty and ambiguity and his own tendency to write up his cases in a fashion that has a quality of certainty, reminiscent of the way in which all the pieces are pulled together when a mystery is solved in a Sherlock Holmes story.

Nevertheless, this emphasis on the importance of the discipline of maintaining an open and receptive attitude can be found in the writings of various analysts subsequent to Freud, including Theodor Reik (1948), Wilfred Bion (1970), to some extent Donald Winnicott (1958, 1965), and recently such analysts as Thomas Ogden (1994) and Christopher Bollas (1992). The emphasis is on maintaining an open, receptive mind that takes in information not just from the client but also from one's own unconscious experience. There has been a shift in recent years toward the importance of being cautious regarding the dangers of approaching the client with an overly tight or coherent formulation that does not easily lend itself to revision in the face of new information. This is particularly evident in the work of some British Independent theorists (e.g., Bollas, 1992; Coltart, 2000; Parsons, 2000) and in the writing of American relational thinkers who emphasized the importance of learning from one's client and being receptive to acknowledging one's own ongoing contributions to enactments (Aron, 1996; Bromberg,1998; Mitchell, 1988, 1993, 1997).

Donnel Stern (1997, 2010), for example, argued that a good psychoanalytic process involves (what philosopher Gadamer referred to as) a fusion of horizons in which both client and therapist come to a shared perspective on reality by allowing themselves to be influenced by each other. An important thread in contemporary theory emphasizes that one can never have an objective understanding of how the other is, because any understanding that develops will inevitably be influenced by the enactment in which one is engaged. Philip Bromberg (1998, 2006) emphasized that there are limits to what one can learn about one's clients on the basis of their verbal reports because they themselves are not able to verbalize aspects of their experience that are split off or dissociated. From this perspective, the only way to truly understand our clients is to enter into their relational worlds and play out various scenarios with them in an unconscious way. Clients who have dissociated their experience are often able only to communicate it through their actions. It is thus only by allowing ourselves to be used by our clients in this way and experiencing and reflecting on our own countertransference that we are able to make contact with dissociated aspects of their experience. The notion that we could have an adequate and comprehensive formulation of our clients prior to actually establishing a relationship with them and allowing our understanding to emerge out of these relationships is anathema. In a more traditional perspective, the therapist's adequate formulation of clients' core themes and psychodynamics allows them to make accurate interpretations, which in turn leads to change through insight. In contrast, the perspective I have outlined suggests that understanding, relating, reflecting, and communicating about what is taking place in the therapeutic relationship are all part of one seamless process.

## Empathy

Empathy is a fundamental factor that is both clinically powerful itself and affects the usefulness of all interventions. The ability to identify with our clients and immerse ourselves in their experience is critical in the process of establishing an alliance. This capacity to identify ourselves with our clients and communicate our empathic experience to them is a central mechanism of change in and of itself. It also has a strong influence on the way that clinical interventions are experienced. As discussed next, the same words of interpretation could be heard very differently depending on how empathically they are delivered. The topic of empathy was traditionally neglected in psychoanalytic writing, in which the emphasis was placed on the importance of making accurate interpretations. With Heinz Kohut and the development of self psychology, however, the topic of empathy was placed in the foreground. Kohut argued that it is not enough for an interpretation to be "accurate"; it also has to be experienced as empathic by the client.

Kohut highlighted the importance of what he termed *vicarious introspection*, that is, the process of placing oneself in the client's shoes and attempting to develop a sense of the client's phenomenological experience. In addition, he emphasized the role that the therapeutic process of empathic mirroring can play in helping clients to develop a cohesive sense of self (Kohut, 1984). The growing influence of mother–infant developmental research on psychoanalytic thinking has added to the analytic perspective on empathy. For example, Daniel Stern's (1985) research on affect attunement in mother–infant relationships has provided a model for understanding the way in which the therapist's ability to attune and resonate to the client's affective experience can help the client to articulate and make sense of his or her own emotional experience.

## Interpretation

One of the most important interventions at the psychoanalytic therapist's disposal has been what is called *interpretation*. An interpretation is the therapist's attempt to help clients become aware of aspects of their unconscious intrapsychic experiences and relational patterns. From a more traditional perspective, the distinction between interpretation and empathic reflection can be conceptualized in the following fashion. Whereas empathic reflection is the therapist's attempt to articulate meaning that is implicit in what the client is saying, interpretation is the therapist's attempt to convey information that is outside of the client's awareness.

There is an important distinction between the accuracy of an interpretation, the extent to which it corresponds to a "real" aspect of the client's unconscious functioning, and the quality or usefulness of an interpretation, in that the client can make use of the interpretation as part of the changes process. An interpretation can be accurate without being useful. The dimension of quality is spoken about in a variety of ways— for example, timing (Is the context right? Is the client ready to hear it?), depth (To what extent is the interpretation focused on deeply unconscious material vs. material that is closer to awareness?), and empathic quality (To what extent is the interpretation delivered in a way that is sensitive to the impact it has on the client's self-esteem? To what extent does it contribute to the client's experience of being genuinely understood?).

Traditionally, interpretations have been conceptualized as falling at different levels along the continuum of depth to surface. A deep interpretation is one targeted at material that is deeply unconscious for the client. An interpretation that is closer to the surface end of the continuum is targeted at experience that is almost accessible to consciousness, but not quite. From this perspective, an empathic reflection can be conceptualized as an interpretation targeted toward the surface end. Although it is often true that the most useful interpretations are those that are close enough to conscious awareness for the client to be on the verge of articulating them, it is important not to rule out the potential value of deeper interpretations. For example, one of the hallmarks of a Kleinian interpretation has been that it is often geared toward interpreting deeply unconscious material that is remote from the client's experience.

It is not uncommon for clients to complain about experiences with therapists who have made deep interpretations that made no sense to them and were experienced as frightening, overwhelming, or disturbing. Nevertheless, it has been my experience that deep interpretations of this sort can be experienced as helpful by clients, especially when the therapist is able to address unconscious anxieties and primitive unconscious fears (e.g., fears related to destructive rage and aggression or annihilation of the self) that feel too unbearable for the client to tolerate. In situations of this type, a therapist's ability to approach unbearable experience in a confident way without feeling overwhelmed can feel reassuring and containing to the client. Here the quality of the therapist's presence and state of mind while making the interpretation is a critical factor. In other words, the therapist's willingness to touch on nameless dreads without being overwhelmed by whatever feelings they stir up can provide the client with a sense of safety and security that typically eludes the client.

Elyn Saks (2008), in a memoir of her personal struggle with schizophrenia, spoke about her experience with a skilled Kleinian analyst (whom she called Mrs. Jones) who helped Saks with her interpretations of the role that factors such as Saks's deep unconscious envy and her projection of angry and hostile feeling onto others play in producing her psychotic symptoms. To quote Saks,

> I met with Mrs. Jones three times a week. . . . I reported my delusions and the forces beyond my control that were unbearably evil. I was malicious, I was bad, I was a destroyer of worlds. She was not afraid; she did not look at me with alarm in her eyes. She did not judge,

she only listened, and reflected back to me what she heard telling me what *she thought it meant* [italics added]. (p. 185)

Following is a dialogue between Saks and Mrs. Jones.

**Mrs. Jones:** Tell me about your difficulties at university.

**Saks:**[1] I'm not smart enough. I can't do the work.

**Mrs. Jones:** You were first in your class in Vanderbilt. Now you're upset about Oxford because you want to be the best and are afraid you can't be. You feel like a piece of shit from your mother's bottom.

**Saks:** I'm closing the curtains from now on because people across the street are looking at me. They can hear what I'm saying. They are angry. They want to hurt me.

**Mrs. Jones:** You are evacuating your angry and hostile feelings onto those people. It is you who are angry and critical. And you want to control what goes on in here.

**Saks:** I *am* in control. I control the world. The world is at my whim. I control the world and everything in it.

**Mrs. Jones:** You want to feel in control because in fact you feel so helpless.

According to Saks (2008),

> While the content of what Mrs. Jones said to me was not always a comfort (more often than not it, it was startling, and had the effect of catching me up short), her presence in the room was. So calm, so reasonable, no matter what I said to her, no matter how disgusting or horrible, she never recoiled from what I said. To her, my thoughts and feelings were not right or wrong, good or bad; they just were. (pp. 92–93)

---

[1]Although this dialogue is quoted from Saks (2008), I have changed Saks's use of the first person "I" to "Saks" to avoid any confusion in the present context.

A number of factors influence the extent to which an interpretation is experienced as empathic. If the interpretation is closer to consciousness for the client, the client is more likely to feel understood because it seems to "fit" or make sense to the client and captures an important aspect of the client's experience that he or she can't articulate. An interpretation that captures or crystallizes a feeling that the client is unable to articulate can be experienced as empathic in the sense that the client feels "known," perhaps in a way that he or she usually doesn't. This is particularly important when the therapist is giving voice to feelings or experiences that are semi-inchoate for the client and contributing to his or her feelings of confusion and isolation.

Interpretations are most likely to be helpful when the therapist is able to interpret a disavowed aspect of experience in a way that the client experiences as validating, supportive, and affirming. For example, a therapist who is able to interpret underlying experiences of sadness and pain and at the same time is able to empathically resonate with these feelings (not just imagine the client's perspective at a conceptual level but also temporarily identify with the experience at a personal and emo-tionally compelling level) will contribute to the client's sense of feeling connected and affirmed. In situations of this type, the therapist's state of mind (i.e., the extent to which the therapist feels empathically connected to the client or not) is just as important, if not more important, than the specific content of his or her interpretation.

When there is a strong therapeutic alliance and the client trusts the therapist, an interpretation that is potentially threatening can be experienced in a more benign way because it is being delivered by somebody whose good will and intention the client trusts. It is also important to bear in mind that the immediate relational context colors the meaning of anything that the therapist says (Mitchell, 1993). Inter-pretations with exactly the same words can be experienced as critical or caring, depending on whether the client feels respected by and cared for by the therapist.

Any intervention must be understood in terms of its relational meaning. In other words, when the therapist makes a specific content interpretation to the client (e.g., "It is hard for you to trust people because of your history of abandonment, and it is hard for you to trust me right now"), the meaning of this particular interpretation will be mediated by the history of the client's relationships with others, by the therapist's unique history, and by the meaning of this type of interpretation to the therapist given his or her particular dynamics and the way both client and therapist are feeling about themselves and each other in this moment. A deep interpretation about the client's unconscious motives may be experienced as disrespectful or disempowering. Alternatively, it may be experienced as tremendously reassuring.

## Clarification, Support, and Advice

Despite the traditional psychoanalytic emphasis on refraining from providing excessive reassurance or advice, many contemporary psychoanalytic therapists find that such support can play a vital role in the change process. Although we do wish to promote our clients' ability to trust in themselves, there is also a recognition that in many circumstances a genuine word of reassurance can be critically important for a client who is struggling with a difficult situation or feeling shaky. Similarly, a word of well-timed advice to a client who is feeling overwhelmed or confused or is in a state of crisis can be an essential intervention. A traditional psychoanalytic concern has been that when therapists give advice or share their opinions with clients, this imposes undue influence on them because of transference and risks compromising their autonomy. Critics such as Owen Renik (2006), however, have argued that the practice of withholding one's opinions as a therapist is disingenuous, because our beliefs implicitly influence the message we convey to our clients without giving them a chance to fully reflect on our position and disagree with us if they wish. A therapist's willingness to give advice, especially when asked for it, is consistent with reducing the power imbalance, because we are "playing our cards straight up" with our clients, but it requires a great deal of self-reflection on the part of the analyst. If analysts are to share their opinions, they must be very aware of the influence of their personal values as well as their countertransferential reactions to the client.

## Interpretation of Transference and Countertransference

Transference interpretations, or those that are focused on the relationship between analyst and client, can be some of the most powerful interventions in psychoanalysis. Exploration of the therapeutic relationship is a hallmark of analytic technique and something that distinguishes it from other forms of treatment. Patients will experience the analyst in a manner that contains aspects of unresolved conflicts with figures in their life, including their early experience with caretakers. Coming to understand this and work through the emotions contained within these relational moments can provide an immediate and impactful experience. Transference interpretations can focus exclusively on the therapeutic relationship or explore similarities between what is taking place in the therapeutic relationship and other relationships in the client's life (both present and past). For example, Doris, a divorced woman in her mid-30s, consistently complains about romantic partners being emotionally unavailable and has just been speaking about her supervisor as not being sufficiently supportive. For the past few sessions I have had the sense that Doris is frustrated with me, so I say, "I wonder if there is any similarity between your experience with your supervisor and the way in which you are experiencing our relationship in this moment?" Interpretations that do not involve a focus on the here and now of the therapeutic relationship can run the risk of leading to a purely intellectualized understanding. It is one thing to conceptually understand one's role in a self-defeating pattern and another to have an emotionally immediate experience of it: the latter is more likely to lead to change.

For many contemporary psychoanalytic therapists, transference interpretations have become inseparable from the process of the exploration of the transference/countertransference matrix. Consistent with an emphasis on a two-person psychology, transference is not conceptualized as a distorted perception arising in a vacuum but as one element in an evolving transference/countertransference enactment. In practice, then, transference interpretations often involve an ongoing collaborative exploration of who is contributing what to the relationship. In my own writing, I have used the term *metacommunication* to designate this process of collaborative exploration (Safran & Muran, 2000). Metacommunication involves an attempt to step outside the relational cycle that is currently being enacted by treating it as the focus of collaborative exploration, a process of communicating or commenting on the relational transaction or implicit communication that is taking place. It is an attempt to bring awareness to bear on the interaction as it unfolds. There are many forms of metacommunication. A therapist can offer a tentative observation about what is taking place between him or her and the client (e.g., "It seems to me that we're both being cautious with each other right now . . . does that fit with your experience?"). A therapist can convey a subjective impression of something the client is doing (e.g., "My impression is that you're pulling away from me right now"). Or the therapist can disclose some aspect of his or her own experience as a point of departure for exploring something that might be taking place in the therapeutic relationship (e.g., "I'm aware of feeling powerless to say anything that you might feel is useful right now"). Any disclosure of this type must be considered the very first step in an ongoing process of exploring the transference/countertransference cycle. The therapist does not begin by assuming that his or her feelings are in any way caused or evoked by the client but rather that they may offer clues as to something that is unconsciously being enacted in the relationship.

It is also important to bear in mind that clients can experience straightforward traditional interpretations of the transference as a criticism, especially in situations in which the therapeutic alliance is strained. In other words, the interpretations can be experienced by clients as the therapist's attempt to take himself or herself out of the equation by insinuating something to this effect: "The tension we're having in our relationship right now is your fault because you are repeating something from your past." This is particularly likely to occur in situations in which the therapist is caught up in an enactment and is using the interpretation to deny any responsibility for what is going on or is defensively blaming the client for a mutually constructed pattern in the therapeutic relationship.

## Nontransference Interpretations

Although I have been emphasizing the value of transference interpretations because of their emotional immediacy, it is important not to minimize the potential value of interpretations that don't make reference to the therapeutic relationship. In some situations, making a well-timed, well-worded interpretation about an event taking place in the person's relationships outside the therapy situation can be particularly useful. This is especially true if the client is curious about what is taking place in the situation and is receptive to considering the possibility that a specific unconscious conflict is playing a role. For the interpretation to be helpful, however, the client does need to experience the interpretation as a new and emotionally meaningful way of looking at the situation rather than just as an intellectualized and arid attempt to understand what is going on. It is difficult to specify exactly what facilitates this sense of newness other than to say that the client needs to be experiencing a genuine sense of confusion and a search for understanding, and the interpretation must be phrased in such a way that it facilitates further exploration rather than shutting down. For example, Peter, a successful professional in his 40s, began treatment after his wife discovered that he was having an affair with a female coworker and threatened to leave him. He immediately ended the affair and sought therapy in the hope of understanding what had led him to have an affair in the first place. This was the only time he had ever had an affair, and he experienced it as completely out of character and a form of compulsion or addiction over which he had no control. After spending several sessions getting to know him, I began to get a sense of a man with considerable disowned anger who was feeling devalued by and emotionally isolated from his wife. I began to interpret his affair as an attempt on his part to reaffirm his sense of potency and lovability and as an expression of disowned anger at his wife. He experienced this interpretation, combined with the process of developing greater ownership of his needs for validation and for emotional intimacy and of his anger, as extremely helpful.

## Genetic Transference Interpretations
## and Historical Reconstruction

A third major type of interpretation is referred to as a *genetic transference* interpretation. A genetic transference interpretation involves conveying a hypothesis about the role that developmental experiences have played in shaping current conflicts. For example, the therapist may interpret the client's tendency to be overprotective of other people, thereby denying his or her own needs, as stemming from the client's history of protecting a depressed and fragile mother. The therapist could look for ways that this history is playing out in the therapeutic relationship and be sensitive to the client trying to put the therapist's needs first. Understanding the effects of childhood relationships on current patterns is particularly powerful when they can be found in the transference and explored in an affectively alive manner through a mutual exploration of the therapeutic relationship.

There has been a tendency in psychoanalytic thinking to emphasize the importance of childhood-based interpretations. The problem is that such interpretations can lead to an intellectualized understanding of the influence of the past on the present without resulting in a real change. Notwithstanding this potential problem, a good genetic interpretation can play a valuable role in helping a client to replace a sense of confusion and perplexity with a sense of meaning and understanding. It can also help to reduce the client's tendency to excessive self-blame by helping the client to see that current patterns are a meaningful and understandable result of an attempt to cope with a difficult or traumatic childhood situation. For example, Howard, a male client in his mid-20s, experienced a lack of direction in his life, a chronic low-level depression, and a sense of inadequacy. His father was an extremely successful business executive whom my client described as charismatic and always the center of attention. When Howard was 8 years old, his father and mother divorced. Although Howard maintained a relationship with his father, he felt he was never able to obtain his approval. Over time, it emerged that whenever Howard would tell his father about something he had accomplished or was excited about, he had the impression that his father belittled him.

In one session, I suggested to Howard that perhaps his father felt the need to "put him down" because of his own need to be the center of attention and an associated feeling of being threatened by any success his son might have. Howard found this interpretation extremely helpful, and it opened the door for exploring important associated feelings, including those that occurred in the therapeutic relationship.

Of course, too much emphasis on tracing the historical roots of one's current self-defeating patterns can lead to a type of preoccupation with the past and a tendency to blame others rather than to develop a sense of agency that can promote change. This is, however, by no means inevitable, and to the extent that it does take place, it can and should be explored in the same way that any defense is explored.

## The Use of Dreams

Dream interpretation has been considered central to psychoanalytic practice since its origins. Freud (1900/1953) referred to dreams as the "royal road" to the unconscious (p. 604), and some of his most important early breakthroughs in psychoanalytic theory and practice emerged from the interpretation of his own dreams and the dreams of analysands. Freud considered dreams to reflect unconscious wishes that seek expression but are felt to be unacceptable to the dreamer; the underlying wishes are the latent content of the dream. The mind represses and transforms the dream content so that it is less anxiety-producing, which yields the manifest content: the dream that the individual actually experiences or recalls. It is through "secondary revision" that primary process material, which is raw and unguarded, is made more acceptable to the dreamer. By deciphering the dreamer's associations to the manifest content, an analyst can get at the original wish or fear or impulse. This idea that true feelings are disguised within symbolic representations underlies many psychodynamic techniques, but because dreams are involuntary and understood to be surreal, the repressed wish may be more easily accessed in this realm.

In *The Interpretation of Dreams*, Freud (1900/1953) outlined a few properties of dreams that, when applied to the content, can aid in their interpretation. Freud noted that events or people from the previous day can show up in the dream; he referred to this as the *day residue*. Freud also noted that the dreamer will often use displacement as a form of disguise—feelings that are held toward one person are expressed in the dream as being toward another. For example, a patient may report having had a dream of fighting with an old schoolmate and wonder why such an insignificant person showed up in their dream. When asked to associate about this schoolmate, the patient thinks of their own brother, and it becomes clear that the feelings the patient experienced are about the brother.

Freud also referred to symbolic representation as a central way for the dreamer to disguise the impulse behind the dream. This is where specific dream content stands in for a deeper issue or conflict. From an analytic perspective, we know that symbols will have personal meaning for each individual depending on their life experience, but in many cultures dream images are taken to have a fixed significance. For example, dreaming of water may be culturally viewed as predictive of turmoil. Although Freud sometimes used the concept of universal symbols, he mostly believed that the unconscious meaning of any particular dream element could be arrived at only by asking the patient to free associate and tell the analyst what comes to mind. This is consistent with the way dream images are understood in current psychoanalytic practice. Any particular element could have a wide range of meaning to the dreamer, which could be understood only with detailed inquiry.

Since Freud's time, a variety of psychoanalytic models have been developed for conceptualizing the meaning of dreams and working with them. One particularly useful approach to dream interpretation was developed by Fairbairn, who conceptualized all figures in a dream to represent different aspects of the self. For example, I once had a female client who was terrified to sleep at home alone when her husband was away. At such times it was common for her to have dreams in which she was being chased by an ax murderer. When I suggested that she experiment or play around with the possibility of seeing herself in the role of the ax murderer, she was able to contact some of the aggressive feelings associated with being in the role and ultimately to contact disowned feelings of anger toward her husband for abandoning her during his frequent business trips.

Dream interpretation is no longer as central to contemporary North American psychoanalytic theory and practice as it once was, but most psychoanalysts do find it useful to work with dreams. Dreams can be particularly helpful when clients have difficulty contacting and expressing their inner life during treatment. In this situation, suggesting to clients that they begin to pay attention to and write down their dreams is a way of providing material for the treatment that emerges spontaneously while the client is asleep and is not subject to the same type of defensive processes that can otherwise drastically constrain the range of experiences. Of course, the client's recording of the dream and subsequent recounting of it in the session involve a process of reconstruction, but the fashion in which it is reconstructed can be of interest in and of itself. Working with dreams can also be particularly interesting when the client reports a particularly vivid dream or one with striking or startling imagery and associated affect. Often these dreams touch on a key issue for the client and can involve their feelings about the analyst and the treatment.

When listening to dreams, I try to avoid any preconceptions about what different aspects of dreams may symbolize or preconceived ideas as to how to work with them. I attempt to listen to the dream with receptive openness and pay attention to both the client's way of talking about the dream and fluctuations in the client's emotional experiences during the recollection. I often stop the client at specific points and ask what he or she is experiencing. I may start by asking what the client thinks of the dream and request associations to dream elements. Sometimes his or her interpretation makes perfect sense to me, and sometimes I find that the ideas that pop into my mind are radically different from the client's formulation. At such times I am curious about the large discrepancy between our interpretations; I may relay some of my own thoughts and ideas and explore how the client responds.

Perhaps most important, I emphasize to clients that there are infinite ways of interpreting any dream and that dream material allows us an opportunity to engage in a kind of interactive play, during which we can experiment with different ways of looking at things and explore how these different alternatives influence both of our understandings. I view dream work as a kind of co-constructive process that allows clients and therapists to engage in a playful way of working with the material. This type of play makes use of intuition and the ongoing process of mutual influence that is taking place as a vehicle for creating meaning together in a way that is not constrained by the type of logical, linear thinking that conversations about clients' everyday experience often are. And as is always the case, I pay particular attention to aspects of the dream that could be construed as referencing our relationship or me (referred to as *allusions to the transference*). I provide a clinical illustration of this process later, when I discuss the case of Simone, a young woman whom I saw in long-term psychoanalytic treatment.

## Working With Resistance and Defense

Almost from the beginning of psychoanalytic thinking, the interpretation of resistance and defense was viewed as a vital technical issue. Ego psychology was particularly interested in exploring the various ways in which the ego plays an active role in defending against unconscious impulses. A central axiom in the ego psychology tradition is that analysis proceeds from surface to depth. In other words, we always begin by analyzing the client's resistances and defenses and only gradually more toward interpreting underlying impulses, fantasies, and wishes as they become more accessible through the process of resistance analysis. As previously discussed, from a psychoanalytic perspective the exploration of resistance is intrinsic to the change process. Clients inevitably have conflicting feelings about changing, and these conflicts manifest in a variety of ways at different points in the treatment. Moreover, resistance stems from an infinite number of different sources (e.g., fear of changing, fear of loss of self, avoidance of painful feelings, negative feelings about the therapist or the therapeutic process, the need to individuate from the therapist, secondary gain [i.e., benefits resulting from maintaining the current symptoms], attachment to old patterns of relating, fear of losing the unconscious, symbolic connection to one's attachment figures).

Common ways in which resistance is expressed in treatment include coming late for sessions, missing sessions, extensive periods of silence or uncommunicativeness, filling the session with superficial chatter or social conversation, failure to pay fees, overcompliance, and what is referred to as a "flight into health" (i.e., experiencing a rapid and transient reduction in one's symptoms as a way of avoiding exploring deeper issues). Some actions facilitate progress in some contexts but may function as resistance in others. For example, the client's reporting of dreams may be an important way of deepening the therapeutic process by communicating feelings and themes that are not consciously accessible to the client. But a client who ritualistically begins every session by reporting dreams may be avoiding the exploration of important feelings or themes in the here and now.

## Defense Interpretation

Innumerable articles and books have been written about the technique of defense interpretation. As I have just discussed, defenses can be named and classified, although this does not capture the dynamic nature of working them through with a client. The following brief descriptions relate how to work clinically with defenses.

The therapist conveys the rationale for interpreting defenses as part of the process of establishing an alliance around the task of defense analysis. For example, I might say to my client,

> People often find ways of avoiding feelings, thoughts, wishes, or
> fantasies that are threatening to them as a way of avoiding distressing
> feelings such as pain or shame. For example, sometimes people have
> difficulty staying in contact with feelings of sadness because of a fear
> that they will be overwhelmed by them or that they will never pass.
> One of my jobs as a therapist will be to help you become aware of
> times that you are doing this, as well as how you are doing it, so that
> you have more of an ability to choose whether you are willing to stay

with a particular feeling, fantasy, or wish instead of unconsciously avoiding it. A fuller awareness of these aspects of your experience will help you to develop a better understanding of what's motivating your actions and will also potentially provide you with important information that helps us understand more fully what things really mean to you and what you're really wanting in any given situation.

Once a rationale has been conveyed to the client, the therapist begins the task of monitoring the various types and ways in which the client cuts off or avoids his experience and begins the process of drawing his attention to avoidances or defensive maneuvers. For example, "I notice that as you talk about your wife leaving you, your voice becomes very even, and you begin to talk in somewhat of a monotone. Do you have any awareness of this?"

Sometimes the client is able to become aware of the defensive maneuvers the therapist is attempting to immediately draw attention to, and the therapist can then follow up with questions such as the following: "Any sense of what was going on in inside of you at that moment?" or even more directly, "Any awareness of avoiding anything in this moment?" If the client is able to become aware and begin to explore an internal experience, the therapist can then follow up with probes such as, "Any sense of what might be difficult about focusing on these feelings?"

In situations in which clients are not able to initially become aware of their defensive maneuvers, it can be helpful to reiterate the rationale for exploring defenses and then remind them that you will try to direct their attention to them when they occur again. By continuing to draw clients' awareness to their defenses as they occur in the present moment, the likelihood of their observing them in real time is increased. This provides clients with an opportunity to attend to the moment and engage in an experientially based discovery process rather than merely speculating. Therapists can help clients to explore what the processes are through which they defend against their experience (e.g., feeling spaced out, changing topics, intellectualizing) and what the unconscious fears, beliefs, and expectations are that prohibit the experience of certain feelings, wishes, and fantasies.

Over time the process of defense interpretation has become more exploratory, dialogical, and collaborative in nature and less "interpretive" (in the sense of therapists simply pointing out clients' defenses to them). The term *exploration of defenses* rather than *defense interpretation* thus is more accurate. There is no simple road map to indicate when a client is avoiding emotions, and the therapist has to have an understanding of the individual. Thus, for example, a preoccupation with talking about the past can sometimes serve as a defense against exploring the present. Other times a focus on the present can serve as a defense against exploring the past.

In addition, it is worth noting that although it is important for therapists to always attend to the style and manner of the client's presentation and to engage in an ongoing assessment of the extent to which he or she is contacting or avoiding an emergent experience in the moment, it is not always advisable to interpret or explore defenses whenever they take place. Sometimes the process of exploring defenses is experienced as too confrontative or critical by clients and can interfere with their ability to contact their experience at a pace that feels safe to them. In other words, sometimes clients need the therapist to support their defenses or to ally with them in order for them to feel safe enough to begin disclosing their inner experience. Defense interpretation should thus be used tactfully, sparingly, and judiciously.

### Working Through Therapeutic Impasses

There is a growing emphasis in psychoanalytic literature on the theoretical and technical importance of working through therapeutic impasses when they emerge (*cf.* Safran & Muran, 2000). Over time the emphasis has shifted from a perspective in which impasses in the therapeutic process are viewed as a function of the client's resistance to one in which impasses are viewed as a two-person interactive process in which client and therapist become locked into a complementary "doer or done to" position from which it feels impossible for either to escape. Benjamin (2004), Davies (2004), and Aron (2006), among others, have written eloquently about how there are times in the treatment process during which both client and therapist are trapped because neither is able to acknowledge the possible validity of the other's perspective without feeling that they themselves are wrong or bad in some fundamental and unacceptable way. For example, the client accuses the therapist of being critical, and the therapist feels that he is being abused by the client. Although it might be possible for the therapist to mouth the words "Yes, you're right, I'm feeling critical," the problem is that he doesn't really experience himself that way, and therefore it would be impossible for him to acknowledge it in a genuine fashion.

In situations of this type, neither client nor therapist is able to truly acknowledge the validity of the other's perspective because it feels that doing so would involve a kind of self-violation or compromise of his or her own integrity. How can the interaction begin to shift out of a frozen position in which there is no alternative to either (a) the client's perspective being valid and the therapist's perspective being unimportant or lacking validity or (b) the therapist's perspective being valid and the client's perspective being invalid or unreasonable? The therapist's task is to facilitate a movement to a third position (i.e., an alternative to the binary choice of "You're right and I'm wrong" or "I'm right and you're wrong"). This process requires an internal shift within the therapist that has a quality of "surrendering" or "letting go" of a position he or she needs to hold on to tenaciously because of underlying and sometimes unconscious fears or threats of acknowledging dissociated aspects of self-experience (Safran & Muran, 2000). For example, perhaps the therapist in the first illustration finds it too threatening or intolerable to experience aspects of himself that are indeed mean. Perhaps this therapist is threatened by fully acknowledging to herself complex feelings of anger and shame around the experience of "being taken advantage of."

To the extent that therapists are able to acknowledge and accept dissociated aspects of their own experience, they begin to experience the psychological freedom to fully appreciate and empathize with the validity of the client's subjective experience without experiencing an internal compromise or a sacrifice or submersion of their own subjectivity. This shift thus involves a movement toward a type of intersubjectivity, in which one is able to experience the other as a subject rather than an object while holding on to one's own subjectivity (Benjamin, 1988, 1990, 2004).

## Termination

Termination is one of the most important phases of treatment. A well-handled termination can play a vital role in helping clients to consolidate any gains that have been made in treatment. Conversely, poorly handled terminations can have a negative impact on the treatment outcome. In a treatment that is not time limited, the topic of termination can be initiated by either client or therapist. Ideally, by the time termination takes place, the client and therapist will have spent some time talking openly and constructively about the process, and the decision to terminate will be mutual. Often clients who are contemplating termination will have difficultly bringing it up directly, and it is important for the therapist to be attuned to cues that the client may be considering ending treatment. For example, the client begins to consistently arrive late for sessions or cancels sessions, seems less engaged in treatment, or asks general questions about how long people typically stay in treatment.

Termination in open-ended treatment is often somewhat messier than the idealized way it is presented in many textbooks. Often termination is the result of extraneous factors (e.g., the client moves to another city). When the factors leading up to termination are not extraneous, it is more common for clients to initiate termination than therapists. This may be because therapists can have more ambitious goals for change that are guided by theoretical concerns, or it may be because the client becomes dissatisfied with the treatment. There are also occasions when both client and therapist feel that the client has achieved the initial therapeutic goals, and the client is the first one to recognize this and to bring it up. When the client brings up the topic of termination in a fashion that feels premature or precipitous for the therapist, it is important for the therapist to carefully explore the client's reasons for wishing to terminate. Sometimes, for example, the client initiates the topic of termination because of feelings of dissatisfaction with the treatment or anger or disappointment with the therapist but has difficulty bringing this up directly. In such situations it is the therapist's task to provide a climate that maximizes the client's sense that the therapist is genuinely interested in and receptive to hearing any concerns about the treatment that the client has and that it is safe to talk about negative feelings or concerns. The subject of termination may be a peek into the client's experience of an enactment that they have been reluctant to discuss. The therapist needs to convey respect for the client's right to privacy, respect for the validity of his or her ultimate decision, and curiosity about what this may mean in light of the client's particular issues.

An important thread to analytic work involves looking beneath the surface explanation to find deeper meaning or unconscious motivation. If the therapist explores the client's reasons for initiating termination in a sensitive and respectful manner, with a genuine receptivity to hearing negative or ambivalent feelings about the therapy or therapist, in some circumstances it can lead to the exploration of feelings such as resentment, mistrust, or disappointment, which if listened to empathically can strengthen the therapeutic relationship and lead to the client's recommitment to therapy. However, when the therapist fails to accept the client's stated reasons for wanting to leave and repeatedly attempts to badger the client into admitting feelings or motivations that he or she either doesn't experience or is unaware of, the client can feel undermined, coerced, or pathologized. The therapist thus needs to strike a balance between, on one hand, trying too hard to hold on to a client who wants to terminate and, on the other hand, failing to adequately explore the client's underlying motivations for terminating.

When the process of exploring the client's desire to leave treatment does lead to a final decision to terminate, it is useful to establish a contract to meet for a certain number of final sessions to provide an opportunity to terminate in a constructive fashion. This process of termination involves numerous principles, such as reviewing the changes that have taken place in treatment, constructing a shared understanding of the factors that have led to change, helping the client to recognize his or her own role in the change process, creating a space that allows the client to express a range of feelings about the termination and the treatment (both positive and negative), exploring or interpreting defenses against experiencing these feelings, exploring potentially painful feelings around loss or fear of separation, and exploring any feelings of disappointment with the treatment and accepting them in a nonjudgmental and nondefensive fashion.

## Exploring Ambivalent Feelings in Termination

It is normal for clients who are terminating therapy to have ambivalent feelings about the treatment and the therapist, just as it is normal for human beings to have ambivalent feelings about all relationships. Clients may experience a range of feelings, including gratitude for the changes that they have made in their lives, fear of ending treatment, relief at no longer having to be in therapy, sadness about the loss of the therapist, abandonment, disappointment about the changes that have not taken place, and resentment toward the therapist because of the failure to realize some of their initial treatment goals or other disappointments with the therapy and the therapist. These feelings are not mutually exclusive. It is important for the therapist to provide a safe place for clients to explore and express the full range of feelings they may have about termination to allow them to obtain a greater degree of closure about the experience of therapy. Some clients may have difficulty acknowledging any negative feelings because of fears (both conscious and unconscious) that they will spoil the positive feelings or hurt or anger the therapist. Other clients may have difficulty contacting and expressing feelings of gratitude. Owning mixed feelings helps clients to learn to tolerate ambivalent feelings. It is also important for therapists not to shrug off positive feelings expressed by the client. The process of experiencing and expressing gratitude and having it graciously acknowledged by the other is a significant part of the growth process.

## Working Constructively With Countertransference Feelings During Termination

Termination is bound to be fraught with a range of feelings for therapists in the same way as it is for clients. It is inevitable that, as therapists, we want to be helpful to our clients and successful with their treatment. It can be difficult to deal with the discomfort that may emerge when clients are not as pleased with the treatment outcome as we would like them to be. Negative feelings are particularly likely to emerge for the therapist when he has experienced a client who is unilaterally terminating as difficult to work with, especially when the therapist has struggled unsuccessfully in an attempt to meet the client's needs or has been an ongoing object of criticism or passive-aggressive behavior by the client. In such situations it can be difficult for the therapist to tolerate negative sentiments from the client without wanting to blame the client for any lack of progress. This in turn may take work on the therapist's part, either in personal therapy or supervision, to become more accepting of his or her own personal failures and limitations. And yet it is critical to remember that for the client, the opportunity to feel that the therapist failed and to express negative feelings about this without retaliation and without feelings of having excessively hurt or destroyed the therapist may be a valuable part of the change process. For example, it may help the client to know that the feelings of the other do not need to be protected or that negative feelings are not toxic and do not have to be hidden. This in turn can help to free the client internally to ultimately be able to experience feelings of closeness and gratitude toward the therapist and others.

## Cultivating a Climate That Tolerates Ambiguity and Lack of Closure

An important aspect of the termination process involves making sense of the entire experience of therapy and establishing a sense of closure. But it is also important for the therapist to recognize and convey an appreciation for the fact that there are limits to the extent of closure that can be obtained on the journey that the therapist and the client have taken together and on their relationship. The meaning of the time that the client has spent in therapy and the meaning of the relationship that he has developed with the therapist will evolve over time, as the client has other life experiences. The therapist often has a sense that over the course of treatment, certain threads running through the client's life story and way of being in the world have emerged, been more clearly fleshed out, and been made sense of, whereas other threads have remained more vague or elusive. Some themes that play out in the therapeutic relationship and unfold over time, or patterns of relating to one another that are frustrating or troubling, can be worked through constructively and understood in ways that help clients gain a sense of movement and mastery in their life. Other themes are less clearly understood by the end of therapy and remain mysteries that may make more sense to the client in the light of subsequent experiences and changes that occur later in the client's life. Learning to live with ambiguity and a lack of complete closure is a significant developmental achievement. In fact, the empirical research on the topic of wisdom has suggested that this type of tolerance of ambiguity is a more advanced cognitive-affective developmental stage (Sternberg & Jordan, 2005). The cultivation of this ability to tolerate such ambiguity can be an important by-product of therapy, especially if the therapist is able to see the cultivation of this kind of tolerance as one of the by-products of a "good enough" termination.

## CHANGE MECHANISMS

Now that I have discussed principles of intervention, I discuss some of the underlying mechanisms that are hypothesized to be active in the change process. How does change actually take place in a psychoanalytic treatment?

### Making the Unconscious Conscious

Psychoanalytic theory postulates a host of different change mechanisms, and a multitude of new ways of conceptualizing the change process continue to emerge as psychoanalytic theories evolve and proliferate. At the most basic level, there is an understanding that change often has something to do with making the unconscious conscious, or in Freud's (1933/1965) oft-cited axiom "Where id was, there ego shall be" (p. 100). Although

Freud's understanding of the nature of the change process evolved over the course of his lifetime, central to his mature thinking was the idea that we are driven by unconscious wishes that we are unaware of, and this lack of awareness compromises psychological freedom and perpetuates self-defeating behavior. For Freud, we delude ourselves as to reasons for doing things, and this self-deception limits our choice. By becoming aware of our unconscious wishes and our defenses against them, we increase the degree of choice available to us. In a sense, then, we decrease the degree to which we are driven by unconscious factors and assume a greater degree of agency.

Developing an awareness of unconscious motives is one of the earliest principles of change delineated in psychoanalytic treatment. Freud's fundamental assumption was that we are motivated by forces that we are not aware of and that this lack of awareness deprives us of choice. In addition, our motives are complex and often contradictory. In psycho-analytic terms, this is referred to as the *principle of overdetermination. Although we might think we understand how we make choices, there are often a multitude of motives.* For example, an individual cultivates an attitude of humility and self-sacrifice through his exposure to spiritual teachings. The desire to be humble and prize the welfare of others is genuine. At the same time, that stance of humility may mask or partially defend against a need to be recognized as special, and the ethic of self-sacrifice may be partially an expression of a self-righteous desire to be morally superior to the other, combined with disowned anger and aggression. To the extent that we are unaware of our motives, our degree of choice is reduced. We do things for reasons that are opaque to us and are then surprised and disappointed by the results. This contributes to a sense of being a victim rather than an agent. Next I discuss a variety of mechanisms that can aid in the process of self-awareness in treatment.

## Emotional Insight

One of the central methods for making the unconscious conscious is the use of verbal interpretations that give clients insight into the unconscious factors that are shaping their experience and actions. One hopes that this is not merely an intellectual recognition; ideally the client can achieve emotional insight—that is, combining the conceptual with the affective so that the client's new understanding has an immediate quality. It has long been held that one of the key ways of increasing the possibility that the insight will be emotional is through the use of transference interpretations (Strachey, 1934), which leads clients to reflect on their immediate experience of the therapeutic relationship rather than to construct an abstract formulation. In other words, by directly observing the way in which they are construing the present moment and acting in the here and now, clients are able to develop an experience of themselves as agents in the construction/creation of their own experience.

Early on, psychoanalytic insiders such as Otto Rank and Sandor Ferenczi raised concerns about a tendency for some psychoanalysts to veer toward a more intellectualist approach that they felt was of limited value (Ferenczi & Rank, 1925/1956). And there is no doubt that the 1960s maverick psychoanalysts such as Fritz Perls (the founder of gestalt therapy) developed an intensely anti-intellectual stance in reaction to what they saw as the tendency toward overintellectualization in psychoanalysis. In general, my impression is that the contemporary American psychoanalytic sensibility has taken the critique of the intellectualist tendencies of psychoanalysis to heart and has placed an important emphasis on the affectively grounded experiential aspects of the change process.

## Articulation of Feelings and Wishes

The process of articulating feelings and wishes is another key mechanism of change in psychoanalytic treatment. As discussed earlier, emotions are a biologically based form of information about the self in interaction with the environment that are wired into the species through an evolutionary process and that play an adaptive role in the survival of the species. Healthy functioning involves the integration of affective information with higher level cognitive processing to act in a fashion that is grounded in organismically based need but not bound by it. Emotions are associated with wishes, which when experienced and articulated can lead to adaptive behavior. Thus, for example, the individual who has difficulty experiencing anger in an appropriate context may be deprived of information that will help him or her to act in an appropriately aggressive or self-assertive way. An individual who has difficulty experiencing feelings of sadness may have difficulty seeking comfort or nurturance from others.

A variety of intervention principles in psychoanalytic treatment help clients to access emotions and associated wishes that are being defended against. These include the communication of empathy, the interpretation of dissociated experience, and the interpretation or exploration of the defenses that interfere with the experience of potentially adaptive wishes and experience. At a more implicit level, the client's experiencing and expressing feelings and associated wishes in the context of a safe and validating therapeutic relationship can play an important role in challenging the unconscious relational schemas that interfere with the experience of these wishes.

## Creating Meaning and Historical Reconstruction

People often come to therapy with difficulty in the construction of meaningful narratives about their lives. These failures of meaning can include both the lack of a coherent understating of their experience and the presence of self-defeating narratives. It can be helpful to construct a viable narrative account of the role that childhood experiences played in contributing to current problems. Emotional problems often arise from psychological coping strategies that were adaptive and made sense in the context of a dysfunctional childhood situation but are maladaptive in the present context. When this is articulated and understood, a client can become more tolerant and accepting toward himself and begin the process of developing better strategies.

Often the problems that clients bring to therapy extend beyond a concern with specific symptoms to a more pervasive sense of meaninglessness and existential despair. When this is the case, the process of exploring and clarifying their own values and engaging in a meaningful dialogue with the therapist can help clients to reorient themselves and develop a more refined sense of what is meaningful to them. For clients, this process of meaning construction often involves becoming more aware of and articulating the nuances of their emotional experience in the context of the relationship with the therapist so that they can begin to get a sense of feeling more vitally alive and in touch with their inner experience.

## Increasing the Experience of Agency

Clients often begin treatment with a diminished sense of personal agency. They experience themselves to be at the mercy of their symptoms or to be victims of misfortune or of other people's ill intent or neglect. They often fail to see the relationship between their symptoms and their own internal and interpersonal conflicts. As clients gain a greater appreciation of the connections between their symptoms and their ways of being, and of their contributions to the conflictual patterns in their lives, they come to experience a greater degree of choice in their lives and to experience themselves as agents rather than as victims. This growing awareness or understanding of one's personal agency must be experientially based rather than purely conceptual.

## Appreciating the Limits of Agency

Coming to experience a sense of agency is, however, only half the battle. The other half involves coming to appreciate and accept the limits of our agency (Safran, 1999). In a culture that promotes the myth that we can "have it all" if only we drink the right wine or drive the right car, it is easy to feel that if we do the right thing we can have everything we desire. Realizing the limits to agency can be part of the growth process of analysis. Winnicott (1958, 1965) spoke about the importance of what he referred to as *optimal disillusionment* in the maturational process. According to him, as children we begin without a clear distinction between fantasy and reality and with the expectation that our needs will magically be taken care of. As we mature and experience inevitable frustrations and disappointments of living in the real world, we undergo a process of disillusionment. If our parents and our environment are unresponsive to our needs, then this disillusionment can be traumatic and we can lose our inner sense of vitality, possibility, and authenticity. We can become over-adapted to the needs of others and develop what Winnicott (1958, 1965) referred to as a *false self*—that is, a way of being that is responsive to the demands of external reality but that loses contact with an inner sense of vitality and realness. If, however, our parents are sufficiently responsive to our inner needs, then this inevitable process of disillusionment takes place in an optimal or "good enough" fashion, and we surrender some aspects of our childhood fantasies without having the vitality and playfulness of our childhood completely extinguished. Building on Winnicott as well as other sources, some contemporary psychoanalytic writers have spoken about this as an experience of "surrender" in which we are able to let go of the idea that we can have it all and accept things as they are (Aron, 2006; Benjamin, 2004; Ghent, 1990; Safran, 1993, 1999, 2016). This sense of the role of surrender in the psychoanalytic change process comes closer to a paradoxical Eastern perspective on change than to the traditional Western emphasis on change through willpower and determination.

## New Relational Experience and Internalization
## of the Therapeutic Relationship

Psychoanalytic theory emphasizes the role that the therapeutic relationship itself plays as a change mechanism. By acting in a way that is different from the way in which the client's parents did, the therapist can provide the client with a new relational experience that challenges his or her maladaptive relational schemas, working models, or internal object relations. This thread in psychoanalytic theory can be traced back to the 1930s to the work of Sándor Ferenczi (1980a, 1980b) and to a seminal article by James Strachey (1934). In the 1940s, Franz Alexander, a Hungarian analyst who had immigrated to the United States, developed a theory of change that he termed the *corrective emotional experience* (Alexander, 1948). Alexander argued that it was essential for the therapist to develop a formulation of the client's distorted beliefs about the nature of relationships with other people and to then intentionally position himself or herself in a way that challenged it. For example, for the client whose parents were overly intrusive, it might be important for the therapist to be particularly respectful of the client's need for privacy. Alexander's position was extremely controversial at the time, as it was seen by his contemporaries as manipulative. It also hit a nerve among analysts who had always believed that what distinguished psychoanalysis from other therapeutic approaches was its emphasis on discovering the truth rather than on the use of the power of suggestion to heal.

Loewald (1960), in a classic work, also emphasized the therapeutic relationship itself as a mechanism of change, but unlike Alexander he made it clear that he was not advocating for a new technical procedure. Instead, he argued that in the same way that children grow through identifying with their parents and internalizing interactions with them, patients grow through internalizing interactions with their therapists. According to Loewald, the therapist's interpretive activity provides a regulating and integrating function for the client, and it is the client's internalization of this integrative experience with the therapist that leads to change.

Modified versions of Alexander's and Loewald's positions are widely accepted by contemporary psychoanalytic theorists who have argued that the therapist's ability to function as a new object for the client (rather than an old object who resembles his or her parents) is a key mechanism of change (Cooper, 2000; Greenberg, 1986). According to this perspective, clients unconsciously try to replicate the relationships with which they are most familiar even though aspects of these dynamics have caused them pain. For example, the client who had critical or sadistic parents will act in ways that evoke critical or sadistic behavior from the therapist. As discussed earlier, the therapist's task is to gradually disembed from the relational scenario that is being played out so that the therapeutic relationship can ultimately function as a new relational experience rather than a repetition of an old one. In contrast to the notion of the corrective experience, the contemporary perspective does not suggest that the therapist should or can develop an a priori formulation of the type of new relational experience that the client needs and then intentionally play a particular role. Rather, the emphasis is on accepting the inevitability of playing the role of an old object (i.e., being recruited into one of the client's characteristic relational scenarios) and then working toward understanding this enactment together with the client and extricating from this role in order to give the client a different relational experience.

## Affect Communication

There is a basic assumption in psychoanalytic theory that an important portion of the communication that takes place between people occurs at an unconscious level. What exactly is meant by this? References to this notion of unconscious communication can be found in Freud's early technical papers. For example, in one early work, Freud recommended that the analyst turn his own unconscious toward the transmitting unconscious of the client.

> He must adjust himself to the client in the way that a telephone receiver is adjusted to the transmitting microphone. Just as the receiver converts the electric oscillations in the telephone line back into sound waves, the doctor is able, from the derivatives of the unconscious that are communicated to him, to reconstruct the original wish or drive that determined the client's free associations. (Freud, 1912, p. 115)

Contemporary research on emotion has suggested that people are remarkably good at reading others' affective displays without conscious awareness (e.g., Parkinson, 1995). Many contemporary analysts who are influenced by developmental research have argued that early mother–infant communication takes place at an affective, bodily felt level prior to the development of any conceptual or symbolic abilities on the infant's part. Developmental researchers such as Ed Tronick (2007) and Beatrice Beebe (Beebe & Lachmann, 2002) have observed that there is an ongoing process of mutual influence in the nonverbal behavior between mother and infant (e.g., gaze, posture, affective tone), in which both mother and infant communicate with each other through nonverbal language or at a presymbolic level. Our first relational experiences thus take place outside the verbal domain and are symbolized or encoded at a presymbolic level, or as what Lyons-Ruth et al. (1998) called *implicit relational knowing.* Implicit relational knowing is a felt sense that is expressed not in what we say but rather in the way we act and feel in relationships. It is thus a kind of procedural knowledge, a knowing about being in relationships that is not encoded at a linguistic level.

Psychoanalysis provides the opportunity for clients to verbalize implicit relational experiences and reflect on the way in which their prelinguistic, implicit, or unconscious assumptions shape the way they understand relationships, construe other people's actions and intentions, and act in relationships. Furthermore, the affective nonverbal exchange can be curative in and of itself as a new relational experience.

## Containment

One of the most important skills for therapists to develop is an internal skill, rather than a technical one. This internal skill involves attending to our emotions when working with clients and cultivating the ability to tolerate and process painful or disturbing feelings in a nondefensive fashion. How do we help our clients hold on to some sense of faith that things will work out when we ourselves are beginning to feel hopeless? How do we work with our own feelings as therapists when working with an extremely hostile or devaluing patient? How do we work with our own feelings when we begin to feel the same sense of despair that our client feels?

The British psychoanalyst Wilfred Bion (1970) referred to this process as *containment.* According to Bion, as part of the normal developmental process, children defend against feelings that are too threatening or toxic for them to experience by projecting them onto the parent. Bion argued that children (and clients) not only imagine that unacceptable feelings belong to the caregiver or therapist but also exert subtle pressures that evoke the dissociated feeling in the therapist. So, for example, the client who experiences nameless feelings of dread and terror dissociates these feelings and in subtle ways evokes these feelings in the therapist. Bion also theorized that children need their parents to help them process their raw emotional experience and learn to tolerate, symbolize, and make sense of this raw experience.

How do children or clients evoke powerful and sometimes dissociated feelings in parents or therapists? Although Bion did not elaborate on the precise mechanisms, contemporary emotion theory and research suggests that (a) it is not uncommon for people to experience the nonverbal aspects of emotion in the absence of conscious awareness, and (b) as indicated earlier, people are remarkably good at reading and responding to other people's emotion displays without conscious awareness (e.g., Ekman, 1993; Greenberg & Safran, 1987). The process of containment is conceptual and affective in nature. Helping the child or client to put feelings into words is certainly one component of it. The more challenging component involves processing and managing powerful feelings that are evoked in us as parents or as therapists so that our own affective responses can help to regulate the other's emotions rather than to further disregulate them.

## Interactive Affect Regulation

The increasingly influential subject of affect regulation has tremendous implications for therapeutic practice. Beebe and Lachmann (2002) argued that the psychologically healthy individual has the capacity to flexibly move back and forth between (a) using his or her own self-soothing skills to regulate distressing emotional experience and (b) using the relationship with the other to help regulate emotions. The ability to regulate internal emotional states begins in infancy in the relationship with the primary caregiver. It turns out that mother–infant observational research has found that attachment security tends to be associated with a midlevel degree of affect attunement between mother and infant. Not surprising, infants whose mothers are consistently affectively misattuned tend to be insecurely attached. These infants can be overly reliant on the use of self-regulation strategies. These may involve activities such as thumb-sucking or gaze aversion or distraction. Perhaps less obvious, infants whose mothers are consistently affectively attuned tend to be insecurely attached as well. It may be that excessive attunement on the mother's part reflects an anxiety about the infant's independence or separation, or alternatively that excessive vigilance on the infant's part reflect insecurity about the relationship, or both. The pattern of mutual attunement that tends to be associated with attachment security is in the midrange—somewhere between the two extremes of emotional neglect and preoccupation with affective connection.

Self-regulation plays an extremely important role in the individual's functioning from birth onward. Self-regulation consists of various strategies and actions used to manage arousal, maintain alertness, dampen arousal when overstimulated, process and manage various feelings, and make constructive use of affective feedback. Self-regulation plays a critical role in the capacity to pay attention to and engage with the environment. As previously indicated, for infants, self-regulation strategies include activities such as gaze aversion and thumb-sucking. In adults, the activities can be daydreaming, fantasy, symbolic elaboration, defenses, rational self-coping strategies, and self-reassurance.

The ability to regulate one's emotional experience is an important component of healthy development. Infants develop this ability through being part of an interpersonal system in which they have the experience of both influencing and being influenced by the caregiver. For example, the infant cries, the mother soothes, the infant calms down, and the mother in turn feels soothed. It takes time after the infant is born for the caregiver to adapt to the specific temperament and characteristic patterns of shifting mood states of the infant. But over time and through a process of mutual adaptation, a certain predictability in the interpersonal system develops. Each partner in the system transforms and in turn is transformed through a process of moment-to-moment coordination of rhythms of nonverbal behavior. Both partners come to trust the predictability of the system, and this implicit trust allows the infant to become self-regulating, even if the caregiver is not attending at the moment, and at the same time to know how to take comfort from the caregiver when necessary.

Similar processes can be observed in psychoanalysis. For example, James, a 50-year-old lawyer, began treatment with me 1 year after having recovered from serious major depression. Although he was not chronically depressed, this had been his second major depression, and he was eager to begin the process of treatment to reduce the possibility of future relapse. One of the things that impressed me about James early on was his self-contained style. He showed very little emotion in our sessions, and although he seemed eager for help from me, there was another level at which I felt that he had difficulty finding value in anything I said or did. James was an intelligent, well-educated, and thoughtful man who had read much psychology, and there was a way in which he seemed to have all the answers in advance. Over time, as I developed an understanding of his developmental history, I came to speculate that he was excessively reliant on the use of self-regulation skills and had tremendous difficulty making use of relationships with others to regulate emotional experience.

In contrast, Elizabeth presented with a desperate need for soothing, comfort, and reassurance from me. She seemed to have no capacity for emotional self-regulation. Furthermore, although sometimes the things I said or did seemed momentarily reassuring or soothing to her, the effects were always short-lasting. She also had a tendency to express her need for reassurance and comfort from me in an intense, angry, and coercive fashion, as if she anticipated that whatever she needed from me would not be forthcoming. Over time I began to get a sense that Elizabeth's parents had been emotionally misattuned and neglectful and that she had often been left alone in states of overwhelming emotional terror. Without the presence of a containing environment, Elizabeth was not able to develop self-regulation skills, and her desperate attempts to coerce soothing from others reflected both this lack and a pained and angry expectation of continuing neglect by others.

With both James and Elizabeth, part of the therapeutic process involved an ongoing attempt to understand how their styles of self and interactive regulation made it difficult to provide them with what they needed. This attempt included an ongoing exploration of what was happening between us in the therapeutic relationship. It also involved a process of thinking out loud together about how important developmental experiences may have played a role in the development of their current affect regulation styles. Just as important, if not more important, however, was a type of organic process through which our evolving relationships helped me to develop a greater capacity to regulate my own affective experience while we were working together. Simultaneously, James's and Elizabeth's evolving shift in implicit relational knowing allowed them to be more open to what I could provide and to make use of our relationship in ways that they were not able to at the beginning. There was thus a kind of mutual evolving relational dance taking place that allowed both me and my clients to change at the same time.

## Rupture and Repair

Relationship ruptures are part of the human experience. Tronick (2007) demonstrated that in normal mother–infant face-to-face interactions, affective coordination between the two occurs less than 30% of the time. Transitions from coordinated to miscoordinated states and back to coordinated states occur about once every 3 to 5 seconds. Tronick hypothesized that this ongoing process of interactive disruption and repair plays an important role in the normal developmental process. It helps the infant develop an implicit relational understanding that both the self and the other are capable of repairing disruptions in relatedness. This ability allows people to negotiate their ongoing needs for attunement and relatedness throughout the life span and provides them with both the sense of self-efficacy and faith in others to know that interpersonal conflicts and misunderstandings do not have to be catastrophic. In the same vein, working through the inevitable misunderstandings and disruptions in relatedness that take place between client and therapist improve a client's implicit relational knowing.

The principle of relationship rupture and repair has come to assume a central role in the thinking of many psychoanalytic theorists as an important element of the change process. For example, Heinz Kohut (1984) came to see the process of working through the therapist's inevitable empathic failures as a central therapeutic mechanism. From his perspective, when the therapist is able to empathize with the client's experience of having been failed, a process takes place in which clients begin to internalize the therapist's empathic presence and results in a type of structural change for clients that allows them to take over some of the therapist's empathic or mirroring functions. These functions are essential for the individual to be able to maintain a sense of self-cohesiveness.

Along similar lines, I have written about the role that repairing ruptures in the therapeutic alliance can play as a vitally important change process (e.g., Safran, 1993, 1998; Safran, Crocker, McMain, & Murray, 1990; Safran & Kraus, 2015; Safran & Muran, 1996, 2000, 2006). This emphasis on the importance of repairing ruptures in the therapeutic alliance has now received attention from theorists and researchers across a range of therapeutic traditions, and a growing body of empirical evidence supports the between rupture repair and good outcome (Eubanks, Muran, & Safran, 2018; Safran, Muran, Samstag, & Stevens, 2001, 2002).

## Mentalization

In recent years the theoretical and empirical work on affect regulation and mentalization has become increasingly influential among psychoanalysts (e.g., Fonagy, Gergely, Jurist, & Target, 2002). Building on attachment theory and research, Fonagy and colleagues conceptualized the capacity for mentalization or reflective functioning as the ability to see ourselves and others as beings with psychological depth. It is a capacity to go beyond the superficial reality and access and reflect on our own thoughts, feelings, and motivations as well as the mental states of others. As such, mentalization can be thought of as a combination of or perhaps a dialectic between self-awareness and perspective taking (Holmes, 2010).

In this respect, the construct of reflective functioning can be further clarified by elaborating on Benjamin's (2004) previously mentioned conceptualization of intersubjectivity. According to Benjamin, the capacity for intersubjectivity is a developmental achievement that involves an ability to hold on to one's own experience of oneself as a subject with a valid perspective while experiencing the other as a subject with his or her own independent wishes, needs, and beliefs that are important in their own right (Benjamin, 1988, 2004, 2018). To the extent that one has the capacity for intersubjectivity, one is able to access one's feelings, wishes, and desires and accept their fundamental validity while able to appreciate the other as a subject with equally complex and meaningful wishes, intentions, and needs rather than as an object or a character in one's own internal drama. One of the ways that therapy can facilitate change is thus through promoting an improved capacity to mentalize. An improvement in this capacity is significant because mentalization plays an important role in allowing the individual to recognize and accept his or her own feelings and needs while managing the complexity of interpersonal relationships in an adaptive fashion and negotiate the needs of self and other.

How does the therapeutic process lead to an improvement in the client's capacity to mentalize? First, as is the case in a healthy developmental process, the therapist's ability to serve as a secure attachment figure for clients helps clients explore feelings and intentions that have previously been dissociated. Second, the process of exploring the transference and countertransference allows clients to have a greater capacity for mentalization by helping them to become more aware of their internal experience and the way in which their actions impact the therapist's experience. Judicious self-disclosure by the therapist in this context can help the client to develop a greater appreciation of the other's subjectivity.

Third, the process of working through ruptures in the therapeutic alliance (therapeutic impasses) also helps clients to develop a greater capacity to mentalize. It is inevitable that therapists will at times fail to live up to their clients' idealized fantasies of what they can provide (e.g., perfect attunement, magically transforming the client's life). When this happens, the therapist's task is to work through these ruptures constructively and to empathize with the client's wishes and desires even if he or she is not always able to fulfill them. As described earlier, this leads to a type of optimal disillusionment that helps clients to begin experiencing the therapist as good enough (Winnicott, 1958, 1965) and as a real subject rather than an idealized object of their fantasies. At the same time, the therapist's capacity to empathize with the client's unmet needs and wishes helps the client to experience his or her desires as valid even if they cannot be fulfilled (Safran, 1993, 1999).

Finally, when a therapist holds a representation of the client in mind, it helps the client see themselves through their therapist's eyes as separate subjects with their own valid feelings and experiences. Especially in the case of more disturbed clients (e.g., clients with borderline pathology), a growing appreciation that the therapist is able to hold them in mind between sessions or during breaks in the therapy plays a role in helping them develop an experience of object constancy (i.e., they are able to hold on to a representation of the therapist as a real person who cares about them even in his or her absence).

## PRINCIPLES OF LONG-TERM VERSUS SHORT-TERM PSYCHOANALYTIC TREATMENTS

In this section, I discuss the principles of both long-term and short-term psychoanalytic treatment. Although there are important similarities, there are important differences as well. I also provide clinical illustrations of both modalities.

### Long-Term, Intensive Treatment

Although it can be helpful to see an analyst three or four times a week, contemporary culture, with its emphasis on speed and efficiency, does not readily support this type of intense involvement in the work. Health insurance rarely covers intensive treatment, and this limits who can benefit from it. At one time it was believed that frequent sessions per week and long-term treatment were necessary for the transference to develop. These days a more common perspective is that both transference and countertransference are present from the very beginning. Nevertheless, it can take time and frequent contact for more intense feelings that are typically kept out of consciousness to emerge. The more important the therapist becomes in the client's life, the more likely it is that experiences within the therapeutic relationship will have a constructive impact on the client.

I am sometimes asked by students whether it is possible to do real psychoanalytic work that involves the development of intense transferences and the careful exploration of transference/countertransference dynamics when the client comes only once a week. My experience is that it depends on the client. Some clients are able to form a strong alliance with the therapist and also have the capacity to explore intense and conflicting feelings about the therapeutic relationship when frequency of treatment is kept to once a week. With others, this is more difficult, and more frequent contact is important. Some clients simply do not have the psychological and emotional capacity to benefit from this intense exploration of what is taking place in the therapeutic relationship, no matter how frequent their sessions. This does not mean that they cannot benefit from psychoanalysis or psychoanalytically oriented therapy, but it does mean that the exploration of transference/countertransference dynamics cannot be a primary vehicle of change for them.

One of the important features of long-term, open-ended psychoanalytic treatment is a sense of evolving process, discovery, and openness to the emergence of new themes. This stance requires a certain tolerance of ambiguity by both client and therapist. In situations in which the client presents with an urgent need or is in crisis, this type of open-ended approach may be frustrating. In such cases, it is critical for the therapist to be responsive to the client's need to focus on the specific problem in a more active and directive fashion. Once the immediate crisis or sense of urgency has passed, the client may be interested in continuing treatment in a more open-ended manner or alternatively may feel that it is time to terminate treatment. Either way, it is important for the therapist to be responsive to the client's needs.

## Simone: An Illustration of Longer Term Psychoanalytic Treatment

Simone was in psychoanalysis with me; we met three times per week for 4 years. At the start of treatment, she was 26 years old. Simone initially sought treatment because of a "general feeling of emptiness" as well as a moderate problem with bulimia, which involved both binging and purging. She was working in a health food store on a part-time basis and was primarily supported by her father. In college, Simone had majored in fine arts, but at the time she was in treatment with me, she was not doing anything related to her education. She was an extremely attractive, intelligent, and well-dressed African American woman. From the beginning I was struck by her lively and playful manner and her sense of humor. I also began to notice early on a tendency on her part to vacillate between states of narcissistic grandiosity during which she denied any needs or self-doubts and (less frequently) states of openness and vulnerability during which she was able to admit to feeling extremely alienated and lonely.

Simone was brought up in a middle-class family in the suburbs and attended a predominantly White school. When I asked what the experience of being one of the only Black children in the school had been like for her, she denied any feelings of discomfort or of not belonging. She told me that most of her friends throughout her life had been White and that she had never given it much thought. During the course of treatment, we explored whether being in treatment with a White therapist had any significance for her. At first she denied that this was the case, but gradually over time, we were able to examine this issue in greater depth.

Simone had two older brothers and one younger sister. Her father had an MBA and was a business executive. Her mother was a nurse. Simone's father left her mother when Simone was 6 years old. Her father and mother had maintained an on-and-off-again relationship over the years, and her mother had always maintained the hope of reuniting with him. When Simone was a child, her father's presence was very unpredictable. He would periodically (e.g., once every 1 or 2 months) come home to spend a weekend and then invariably leave early after having a fight with her mother. Simone described poignant memories of running down the road after his car, crying. She maintained that initially she would be very excited when she knew that her father would be visiting. Eventually she stopped feeling any excitement (as a form of self-protection) and then transitioned into a third state in which she experienced no feelings but pretended to be excited to avoid alienating her father.

Simone's father continued to be unpredictable in the relationship with her as she grew older; he would periodically contact her, take her out for lunch or dinner, make plans to see her again, and then disappear from her life. When Simone spoke about her father, there was a romantically charged quality. Simone never reported a literal sexual boundary violation in the relationship, and it seemed to me quite possible that there never was one. However, she conveyed a sense of awkwardness and shame about their interactions, and her perception was that her father felt awkward ("as if he was on a date") as well. Another factor contributing to my speculation that there may have been some kind of sexual boundary violation in Simone's childhood was that she sometimes spoke about experiencing a type of "disgusting energy" emanating from her that drove people away (my experience has been that feeling disgusting in some fundamental way is not unusual for clients who had been sexually violated as children). The possibility of a sexual boundary violation having taken place in Simone's childhood was not a topic that we ever fully explored in our work together, but I did wonder whether it may have impacted her way of relating to me and her difficulty in accepting support and nurturance from me.

Simone maintained that when she was a child, her mother had been erratic, alternating between episodes of intense anger and periods of fragility and dependency on her. She remembered learning to be vigilant to shifts in her mother's mood to avoid triggering an outburst. She also remembered learning to take care of her mother emotionally. She described her mother as very emotionally needy and dependent and felt judgmental of her. This critical perspective on her mother contrasted with an idealized view of her father, whom she viewed as independent and with whom she identified.

Simone was extremely shy in school and saw herself as "ugly." Her first romantic relationship was at the end of high school. She was involved with a boy for 1 year but had no sexual relationship with him. When he left to attend college, Simone became briefly involved with his best friend.

On one occasion, she had sexual intercourse with him and found it traumatic. When she described the reasons why she had experienced the event as traumatic, I began to get a sense of some pockets of semi-delusional ideation in Simone's thinking that were generally kept well contained. Simone told me that prior to this incident, she had believed that she would give birth to a child through immaculate conception and that now this could never happen.

After this relationship, she began to have same-sex relationships and was involved with a woman at the start of treatment. Simone's longest romantic relationship (besides her first high school boyfriend) had lasted 1 month. Her typical pattern would be to end romantic relationships when she began to experience her partner as being too "emotionally needy." When Simone began treatment, she did not see the absence of long-term romantic relationships in her life as a problem or as something she wished to change.

Over the course of treatment, Simone and I spent considerable time exploring the factors contributing to her feelings of emptiness, as well as her binging behavior. She fluctuated dramatically (both within sessions and various stages of the treatment) in her ability to look at her own feelings and actions in a self-reflective fashion. But at times when she was feeling safer and more open, she was able to express a desire to improve the quality of her relationships with people, a wish to be in a long-term romantic relationship, and a curiosity in understanding interfering factors. We explored the way in which her father's unpredictability had contributed to the development of a counterdependent stance on her part. In addition, we explored the way in which she had identified with her father (and his apparent emotional aloofness) and repudiated the more vulnerable dependent aspects of herself that she associated with her mother (whom she saw as pathetic). We also explored the way in which her binging was connected to a desire to fill an experience of emptiness inside of her and the relationship between her dissociation of dependent feelings related both to her feelings of disgust when she experienced romantic partners as "needy" and to her own difficulty in allowing others to relate to her in a nurturing fashion.

Simone revealed additional elements of semidelusional ideation (e.g., a belief that certain people she met had special powers, a belief that she could read other people's minds). At such times, Simone disclosed information tentatively and with a somewhat self-deprecatingly humorous style, as if to say, "I don't take this completely seriously." She vacillated in terms of how trusting of me she felt and how willing she was to reveal beliefs of this type. Her fear that I would not understand or could not fully embrace her beliefs was an ongoing focus of discussion.

Throughout the treatment Simone was preoccupied with new age beliefs and ideas; she would spend hours browsing bookstores in what seemed like a desperate attempt to fill what she described as a "hole" or "emptiness" inside her. Inevitably Simone would leave the store feeling unsatiated—bored with the activity and not fulfilled. In time we came to understand this activity as similar in function to her binging behavior (i.e., a desperate attempt to fix an internal experience of emptiness).

A few months after beginning treatment with me, Simone became involved with a cult, and this involvement continued and intensified over the first 2 years of her treatment. An important focus of exploration was her concern that her spiritual interests were incompatible with psychotherapy. In addition, the impact of Simone's dissociated dependency needs emerged more fully in the cult. The allure for her of being able to completely surrender to the cult and its leader became more and more apparent. The prospect of having somebody take charge of her life completely and tell her what to do and what not to do in any given situation was undeniably appealing to her.

As discussed previously, there was a continuous alternation in treatment between periods when Simone seemed quite open and able to engage in an exploratory process and periods when she was highly defended and rejected any attempt on my part to explore underlying feelings or look for deeper meaning. Although these alternating states never completely disappeared, over the course of treatment they became less frequent and intense, and Simone became better able to explore both her internal experience and the meaning of our relationship to her.

At the beginning of treatment I had the sense that Simone had one foot in and one foot out of therapy. She would often miss sessions (claiming that she had forgotten) or arrive 15 to 20 minutes late. For the most part, she would resist any attempt to explore feelings or factors underlying her inconsistent and late attendance. I found myself feeling anxious that she would leave treatment precipitously and concerned that any attempt on my part to explore her ambivalence would hasten her departure. I also found myself feeling concerned that she would experience my attempts to explore her ambivalence as reflecting my own neediness, and I was more hesitant than I usually am to explore a client's ambivalence about treatment as a result. I began to conceptualize what was taking place as an enactment in which Simone's own anxieties about dependency led to a lack of investment in our relationship, which in turn fueled feelings on my part of both anxiety and shame about my insecurity. My own conflicts about dependency and a concern about seeing myself as needy were being triggered by Simone's avoidant style and interfering with my ability to constructively explore Simone's contribution to what was taking place between us.

Over time I became aware of the quality of narcissistic grandiosity in Simone—a belief on her part that she had all the answers and that nobody else, including me, had anything of value to say to her. This attitude is not one that emerged explicitly at first but rather gradually as I became aware of my own countertransference feelings of not being able to say things that she really took in, and I was able to use my feelings as a point of departure for exploring what was going on in our relationship. Gradually Simone was able to acknowledge belief that I did not have anything useful to say to her. She was able to articulate an underlying fear that if she did become more receptive, she would become dependent on me and vulnerable to abandonment. Simone and I were able to collaboratively make sense of her counterdependency and narcissistic defenses in terms of her experiences of abandonment as a child, and she became more open to input from me. A central dilemma that emerged for her was the conflict between, on one hand, fearing dependency on others and feeling that nobody (including me) had anything of value to offer her and, on the other hand, desperately wishing that others would be able to introduce their subjectivity in a way that would help her feel less alone. We explored these themes in a variety of ways throughout treatment. To provide one example, I describe the way in which a dream that Simone reported in the 5th month of our work together led to an exploration of her ambivalent feelings regarding dependency in our relationship and provided hints of her complex feelings about sexuality, men and dependency, and our relationship. She reported this dream shortly after her father had invited her to temporarily move into an apartment he owned, where he would stay periodically when he came to the city on business trips.

**Simone:** I'm with some people on a beach and they're playing with a puppy. And they've got the puppy partially submerged under the water . . . maybe to soothe it. But it's not happy. And so I decide to take over. . . . I see a male dog who I think is its father . . . but it's interesting because this male dog has udders. So I take the puppy and put it on its father's udders, and then the puppy seems happy.

**Safran:** What do you make of the dream?

**Simone:** Well, maybe the dog is actually my father, and maybe it has to do with me moving into his place.

**Safran:** That makes sense . . . and I'm also thinking . . . and this is really just playing around with the images . . . so don't take what I'm saying too seriously, maybe the male dog is me [I say this in a very tentative way, so it will be easy for her to dismiss without feeling too dismissive, but also in an attempt to gauge how capable she is of acknowledging feelings of intimacy and dependency in our relationship at this point].

**Simone:** I hadn't thought of that.

**Safran:** How does it feel?

**Simone:** I don't know. . . . I'd have to think about it.

She then goes on to tell me another dream fragment.

**Simone:** And then in the dream, I see my old advisor from college, Emma. . . . She's a woman, but then I look at her shadow and it's the shadow of a man.

**Safran:** What do you make of it?

**Simone:** I don't know.

**Safran:** I know from what you've told me previously that last time you visited Emma you felt uncomfortable with her because she felt needy to you.

**Simone:** Well, it's like the way she was always trying to look after me and offer me guidance, it felt like there was a kind underlying desperation . . . or neediness . . . like maybe she needs to relate to me as a daughter or something.

I wonder to myself if this might be another reference to our relationship. Perhaps Simone experiences my attempts to help her as representing a form of neediness on my part. But I decide not to explore this potential allusion to our relationship because of a concern that she will find it too threatening. Simone continues talking about the dream at the following session.

**Simone:** I was thinking about that dream I had about that male dog with the udders . . . and it makes me feel uncomfortable.

**Safran:** Are you willing to explore what feels uncomfortable about it? [This is a form of defense analysis.]

**Simone:** Well, there's something yucky about it. I don't really like to think of myself as getting nurtured by you. There's something scary about it.

**Safran:** Scary in what way?

**Simone:** Well, it would mean that I'm dependent on you, and that brings up a whole bunch of feelings.

We continue to explore the range of feelings it brings up: fear, yearning, revulsion, fear of abandonment, and so on.

**Simone:** You're not really a father figure for me. . . . It's like you're not really male. It's like you just exist in my head.

**Safran:** Can you say more about me not being male?

**Simone:** Well, you don't give me advice or tell me what to do.

**Safran:** Would you want me to give you advice?

**Simone:** No.

**Safran:** Why not?

**Simone:** Because then I would become dependent on you. You're not like my father that way. Things are complicated with him.

At this point Simone transitions into talking about her complicated feelings about what she refers to as the "sexual energy" between her and her father. She speaks about how her father always makes it clear to people that she is his daughter when he takes her out to dinner, as if to ensure that no one assumes they have a romantic relationship. She speaks about the fact that on occasion she has slept at her father's place when he is out of town and that she feels uncomfortable sleeping in his bed because she knows that he "entertains people there."

I speculate to myself that it is important for Simone to desexualize me in her mind because the potential of my playing a paternal role with her may have threatening sexual connotations for her. But again, I don't say anything at this point because I feel it would be premature.

The following session, Simone spontaneously brought up the possibility that maybe the male dog with udders in her dream does represent me. We continued to explore what this possibility meant to her during this session, and the intertwined threads of conflict around dependency, sexuality, and romantic relationships with both men and women continued to unfold and become further illuminated throughout the treatment.

Approximately halfway through treatment, Simone became romantically involved with Jim, a 30-year-old African American musician. Jim was the first male Simone had been romantically involved with since her adolescence. Over a period of time Simone was able to genuinely contact her desire for Jim and her hope that things would work out between them. Although Simone was not able to explain her new interest in a romantic relationship with a man, I speculated to myself that perhaps the process of becoming more trusting of me, a male therapist, helped her to begin to experience men in general as safer and less likely to abandon her in the same way that her father had. This possibility was not, however, something I felt Simone was ready to explore explicitly in treatment, so I did not introduce it.

Ultimately Jim rejected Simone. My impression was that she experienced this as excruciatingly painful and subsequently shut down and began again to deny her need for him or for anyone else, including me. She flirted with the idea of leaving both treatment and the city to enter an ashram associated with the cult she had joined. After a futile and extended attempt on my part to explore what was going on for her, I settled into providing more of a supportive, containing environment for her in which I would try to mirror or empathize with the manifest level of her experience. After approximately two months, Simone began to become more emotionally open again, more receptive to exploration, and she stopped talking about leaving treatment.

Subsequent to this, she began dating a number of men and ultimately settled into a relationship with a man named Scott. It was in the context of this relationship that she had sexual intercourse with a man for the first time since her adolescence. She moved in with Scott in a rather precipitous fashion and continued living with him for approximately three months. She struggled with intensely ambivalent feelings about the increased intimacy and fears of dependency and engulfment. We spent considerable time in therapy exploring the difficulty she had in negotiating between his needs and her own, and we explored the parallel between the issues emerging in her relationship with Scott and the transference.

Simone found living with Scott increasingly intolerable, alternating between feeling that he was too needy and very occasionally acknowledging fears of abandonment and rejection. Eventually she left him to move in with another man who was a member of the cult. At the same time, she began to discuss the possibility of leaving treatment again, maintaining that she was feeling better and that she had accomplished the goals she had at the beginning of treatment. I gently and tentatively explored with her the possibility that her wish to leave treatment was motivated (at least in part) by a desire to avoid the type of intensely ambivalent feelings evoked by the intimacy of our relationship. Gradually she came to acknowledge that this was true and then began to settle into a phase of treatment during which she remained considerably more trusting and open for an extended period of time.

Although Simone continued to vacillate between periods of self-reflection and periods of shutting down and emotional withdrawal from me, the intensity of these swings decreased considerably. Also, during this phase Simone substantially decreased her binging behavior and became less preoccupied with eating. She began to work on her art for the first time since ending college and was able to experience this as a source of satisfaction. Simone and I continued to explore her feelings of ambivalence about intimacy and her fear of dependency both in our relationship and in relationships in general. She also began to talk more openly about feelings of being "different" because most of her friends were not Black, and we started to explore ambivalent feelings about being in therapy with a White therapist. We explored the way in which Simone did not feel completely at home in either the White world or the Black world and the way this contributed to her general feeling of alienation and isolation.

In the final 6 months of our work together, Simone became romantically involved with a man named Jamal, and this relationship developed a more stable quality than her previous relationships. Although she was not without feelings of ambivalence, she was better able to tolerate her feelings of dependency on Jamal and was less self-critical of her need for him. She began working more consistently at the health food store and developed a plan to save up enough money to return to college with the help of her father to take some specialized courses in graphic design.

Two months before ending treatment, Simone raised the possibility of termination. This time, however, things had a different feeling about them than they had previously. It was clear to both of us that she had made some important changes in her life, and although it was far from clear what the future would hold in terms of her current romantic relationship or her plans to return to college, there was a mutual sense that she had started on a different path than the one she had been on at the beginning of treatment. We set a termination date in advance and, over the remaining time, explored the ways in which she had changed over the course of our work together and her feelings about termination.

At first she denied any ambivalent feelings about leaving treatment and expressed an eagerness to "do things on her own" now that she no longer needed my help. I wondered to myself whether it might be a bit premature for her to leave treatment and had some concern that she would not be able to maintain the gains she had made. I also wondered whether her plans to terminate were once again related to her fears of intimacy and abandonment and distaste for dependency. At the same time, however, I considered the possibility that my reactions reflected my own reluctance to let go of her and perhaps an overestimation of the significance of my own role in her life. I disclosed some of these feelings to her, and this facilitated an ability on her part to begin to explore some of her ambivalent feelings about leaving treatment. She was ultimately able to acknowledge anxiety about becoming too dependent on me, fears about how her life would go after she left treatment, and—toward the end—feelings of sadness about ending our relationship. When we ended treatment, I made it clear that she was welcome to contact me any time, just to let me know how things were going or to schedule another session if she wished.

I received a letter from her about 2 years later. She wrote that things were basically going well in her life. She had left Jamal approximately 4 months after she terminated with me. Three months later she had become romantically involved with another man, and they were still in a stable relationship. She was working for a small group as a graphic designer and was finding the work challenging but satisfying. Simone wrote that periodically she would still lapse into periods of binging, especially during difficult times. But she wrote that in general, her binging was much more in control than it had been when she began treatment. Overall Simone felt that her treatment with me had been helpful, and I concurred. I had a sense that our work together had reached a depth that allowed her to make some significant changes in her life and significant internal changes as well. I also had the sense that there were many themes left unexplored and that Simone could have benefited from more treatment. It seems possible that she may go into treatment again at some point in her life. At the same time, however, I believe that no story ever completely unfolds in any treatment and that at any given point a specific client and therapist are able to reach the depth and accomplish what they are both ready and able to accomplish at that time.

## Short-Term Treatment

Although psychoanalysis has become almost synonymous with long-term open-ended treatment, brief-term psychoanalytic treatments have a long history and have become increasingly common in the last 20 years. As previously indicated, the original psychoanalytic treatments were not nearly as long as contemporary psychoanalyses. Sándor Ferenczi experimented with a wide variety of active interventions to speed up the process of change, including the establishment of time limits. Ferenczi also collaborated with Otto Rank (Ferenczi & Rank, 1925/1956) to write about the use of active and directive interventions to promote a more rapid and effective treatment. Rank (1929) subsequently experimented with the use of short-term time-limited treatments as a way of mobilizing the client's will and highlighting dependency and separation issues.

Many short-term psychoanalytic or short-term dynamic treatments have been developed. Messer and Warren (1995) categorized existing forms of short-term psychoanalytic treatment into two types: drive/structural and relational. Drive/structural approaches all subscribe to an ego psychological approach and emphasize the interpretation of wish/defense conflicts as a central ingredient of change. These tend to be quite confrontational in nature and by and large assume a one-person psychological perspective, paying little attention to the therapist's contribution to enactments that are taking place. Some of the best-known examples of the drive/structural approach are the approaches of David Malan (1963) and Peter Sifneos (1972).

The best-known variants of the relational approach are the approaches of Lester Luborsky (1984) and Hans Strupp and colleagues (Binder, 2004; Levenson, 2017; Strupp & Binder, 1984). These approaches conceptualize problems as the result of recurrent maladaptive patterns of interpersonal behavior resulting from internal object relations, which are themselves the result of disturbances in relationships with early caretakers. Although these approaches do not preclude an emphasis on wish/defense interpretation, they pay particular attention to the relationship between the interpersonal context of these conflicts and the way in which they occur in the client's everyday life and in the therapeutic relationship.

Although there are important theoretical and technical differences in these two general types of short-term treatments, most share certain features that distinguish them from longer term psychoanalytic treatments. These features include the following characteristics: an emphasis on developing a case formulation early in treatment, the use of this formulation to establish and maintain a focus throughout the treatment, a high level of therapist activity, the establishment of a set number of sessions or a clear termination date in advance, and an emphasis on working through the meaning of termination for the client. In addition, many of the short-term psychoanalytic or dynamic approaches use termination as an opportunity to focus on issues of separation–individuation and loss that are conceptualized as playing a central role for people in their lives.

Because contemporary psychoanalytic practice tends to be long term and open-ended in nature, it is often a challenge for therapists who are trained in a traditional psychoanalytic model to make the shifts in attitude relevant to doing short-term therapy. As Messer and Warren (1995) pointed out, the emotional challenges for therapists include feelings of guilt over not being able to offer the client more, struggling with one's grandiose and perfectionist ambitions in light of the constraints of a short-term approach, and dealing with feelings revolving around separation and termination (e.g., feeling guilty about abandoning or rejecting a client, mourning the end of a meaningful relationship).

Short-term dynamic therapists use many of the interventions used by long-term psychoanalytic therapists, including interpretation of unconscious feelings, wishes, and defenses; interpretation of the resistance; transference interpretations; extratransference interpretations; and genetic transference interpretations. There is often a higher level of therapist activity in short-term dynamic therapy and a likelihood of making more frequent transference interpretations to maximize the impact of the treatment in the short time available. In practice, there is often more of a confrontational nature to short-term dynamic therapies than in many approaches to long-term therapy given the need to speed up the change process. This was particularly true in the first generation of popular short-term dynamic approaches (e.g., Davanloo, 1980; Sifneos, 1972), although more recent developments in the short-term dynamic approach appear to be learning from experience and now place more emphasis on emotional attunement, establishing an alliance, and allowing clients to work at their own pace (e.g., Fosha, 2000; McCullough Valliant, 1997).

As previously indicated, the majority of short-term dynamic approaches attempt to deal with the time constraints by establishing an explicit formulation of a core dynamic theme for the client to serve as a guiding focus for interventions throughout the treatment. The assumption is that this type of focus is essential to make efficient use of the time (Safran & Muran, 1998). Although formulation plays an important role in any psychoanalytic approach, this emphasis on setting up an explicit formulation so early in the treatment is in some respect at odds with the sensibility of a long-term open-ended psychoanalytic treatment that emphasizes the importance of cultivating an openness to the emergent process. In other words, establishing an early formulation is in tension with the stance of evenly suspended attention, which is designed to allow the therapist's unconscious processes and associations to be receptive to the client's associations and the unconscious processes to which they are linked.

An approach to short-term treatment that has been extensively influenced by recent developments in relational psychoanalysis is brief relational therapy (BRT; Muran et al., 2009; Safran, 2002; Safran & Muran, 2000). BRT is an integrative approach that shares a number of similarities with other short-term dynamic treatments, but it is also distinguished by the fact that its development has been substantially influenced by principles emerging out of relational psychoanalysis and by findings emerging from our empirical research program on ruptures in the therapeutic alliance. The key characteristics of BRT are as follows: (a) it assumes a two-person psychology, (b) it involves a focus on the here and now of the therapeutic relationship, (c) it involves an ongoing collaborative exploration of both the client's and the therapist's contribution to the interaction, (d) it emphasizes in-depth exploration of the nuances of the client's experience in the context of unfolding enactments and is sparing in the use of interpretations that draw links between the transference and other relational patterns, (e) it makes use of countertransference disclosure and therapeutic metacommunication, and (f) it assumes that the impact of any intervention is always mediated by its relational meaning. Consistent with a two-person psychology, BRT emphasizes that the therapist's formulation must always be informed by an evolving understanding of the nature of his own participation in relational scenarios that are being enacted with the client. BRT thus places less of an emphasis than many other short-term dynamic approaches on the importance of developing a clear-cut dynamic formulation early in the treatment.

## Amanda: An Illustration of a Short-Term Psychoanalytic Treatment

The case of Amanda provides an illustration of psychoanalytically oriented treatment administered in a highly abbreviated form. This case has some unique characteristics because I treated Amanda for an American

Psychological Association (APA) video illustration of psychoanalytic therapy. Because of the nature of the series, I saw her for only six sessions, which is certainly toward the low end of the continuum (short-term therapies that are typically studied in randomized clinical trials are usually in the range of 12 to 25 sessions). Amanda is someone who would be suitable for longer term, open-ended treatment and given the chronic and severe history of her problems, her history of abandonment (which I discuss shortly), and her potential receptiveness to long-term treatment, I would not normally recommend short-term therapy as the treatment of choice for her.

It is also important to bear in mind that our work together was inevitably influenced by the fact that it took place in a production studio with cameramen and high-tech equipment present and that both Amanda and I were aware that this was not "ordinary therapy" but rather a treatment conducted specifically for purposes of filming a training video. This placed a considerable amount of pressure on both Amanda and me and certainly compromised the type of privacy and safety that under normal conditions are so critical to psychotherapy. On the other hand, my feeling is that the process that unfolded as we worked was sufficiently similar to the process that takes place in a regular psychoanalytic treatment to make it a useful illustration, especially since the video is available from APA and allows for a more detailed examination of the process.[2] Furthermore, the exploration of the impact of the videotaping on the treatment became a central focus of our work, thus allowing for an exploration of the impact of this aspect of the therapeutic frame on the transference and countertransference.

Prior to beginning the process, the video production team asked what type of client to select for the demonstration, and I decided to screen for someone who felt that this seemed like a meaningful way of working. Accordingly, I wrote a statement providing a rationale for psychoanalytic

---

[2]The video which can be accessed at https://www.apa.org/pubs/videos, is titled *Psychoanalytic Therapy Over Time* and is copyrighted by the American Psychological Association. Please note that the client's name and other identifying information have been changed here to protect her confidentiality. The reader who watches the video may notice some discrepancies.

treatment, which was to be given to the client. The rationale emphasized the importance of exploring unconscious feelings and thoughts, examining self-defeating patterns that are enacted unconsciously, and using the therapeutic relationship as a specific focus of exploration to shed light on unconscious patterns that are potentially enacted in other relationships. I mention this here because it became particularly relevant in my third session with Amanda.

Amanda was a young White woman from a working-class background with a history of serious depression and substance abuse. Before seeking treatment with me, she had experienced three serious and incapacitating major depressive episodes, and she claimed that she had been depressed for as long as she could remember. She also had a long history of addiction to both street and prescription drugs. In addition, she had a history of involvement in romantic relationships with abusive men. At the time of our first interview, Amanda had already begun to make some important changes in her life. She had joined Narcotics Anonymous and had been drug free for more than a year. She also had been in remission from major depression for more than a year and was working part time. Her stated goal in seeing me for six sessions was to continue working on developing the psychological resources to change her pattern of self-destructive romantic involvements.

Session 1 with Amanda was spent for the most part gathering information about her presenting problems and goals, history of problems, personal history, and current life situation and level of functioning in an attempt to develop a sense of whether I could be at all helpful to her in this context. I also attempted to lay the groundwork for the establishment of a therapeutic alliance by both empathizing with her and working collaboratively with her to develop a shared understanding of her problem and her goals and how we were going to work toward them. I was also beginning to attend to my own countertransference feelings to see if I could begin to get a hint or a felt sense of what it would be like to relate to her. For the most part, my sense was that things flowed smoothly between me and Amanda in this session. There was a quality of synchrony between us, almost a dance. I felt that I was able to empathize with her and that she was able to take in my empathy.

I also noticed that on the few occasions when I asked Amanda more open-ended questions and allowed her an opportunity to take the lead and elaborate, things started to feel a bit awkward. At these points she would talk about feeling "on the spot," and I found myself automatically rushing in to pick up the slack. It felt as if I had to do this to keep things running smoothly, and I found myself noting these feelings to myself and filing the experience away for potential exploration at some later point.

In the session, Amanda recounted a traumatic childhood. Her biological father abandoned the family when she was 4 years old. Her stepfather (whom her mother married when Amanda was 6 years old) was a firefighter. He was also an alcoholic and physically abusive toward her mother. She had memories of her stepfather coming home in a drunken rage, getting into arguments with her mother, breaking furniture, and hitting her mother. When these episodes would occur, Amanda recalled playing the role of the mediator, trying to break up the fights by actually placing herself physically between her mother and stepfather and separating them. Amanda remembered that at one point when she was 9 or 10 years old, she had called the police to break up the fight and that her mother had to be taken to the hospital. In contrast to this physical violence toward her mother, Amanda claimed that her stepfather was never abusive toward her. She described him as her "best friend when sober." Amanda's stepfather committed suicide when she was 15, and over the years she had a whole range of feelings about this: guilt for not being able to save him, hurt, anger, betrayal, and abandonment.

In this session, I began to have a preliminary sense of interpersonal themes in Amanda's life that might be relevant to developing a working formulation. I began to wonder if abandonment was a recurrent issue in her life. I also began to think about her role as the mediator between her mother and her stepfather. It's not unusual for this type of developmental experience to lead to parentification and a precocious maturity as children in this position feel helpless and abandoned and simultaneously feel special and empowered by their role in the family dynamics. But these feelings of power and specialness are often hidden or partially unconscious. This type of experience can thus lead to the development of a way of being with others in which an individual adapts by learning to take care of other people's needs rather than his or her own (what Winnicott, 1965, referred to as a *false self* organization). This can develop into a sense of overwhelming personal responsibility, difficulties in truly depending on others, and unconscious or semiconscious feelings of both grandiosity and resentment.

Despite her traumatic background and history of serious psychological problems, Amanda had a number of significant emotional and psychological strengths. She was intelligent, had completed an undergraduate college degree, and had a network of friends she could rely on (through Narcotics Anonymous). I was also beginning to get a glimpse of a feisty and lively side to her and a sardonic sense of humor, which intrigued me. By the end of our first session, I found myself admiring Amanda's strength, resilience, and feistiness. I also found myself deeply concerned about her and wanting to help her. At the same time, I sensed a hint of underlying wariness or mistrustfulness in her. Although our first session went relatively smoothly, I wondered to what extent this smoothness would continue over our time together.

In our second session, the dynamic that had begun to emerge between Amanda and me in subtle ways started to come through more clearly. I sensed that as long as I was taking the lead and asking her factually oriented questions, things would continue to go relatively smoothly. And I found myself doing this reflexively, while continuing to make a mental note of it, wondering where it was leading. I began the session by continuing to collect background information. I asked about her relationship with her mother and her biological father (whom she had gotten to know again as an adult), in part because I felt it could provide context for her difficulties but also perhaps partially because I sensed that a more active stance on my part would help to maintain Amanda's anxiety at a manageable level and help to build the alliance.

At the same time, I was beginning to develop a vague sense that there may have been something a little off about the quality of Amanda's affective engagement in the session. I found myself wondering if she was talking about something that was emotionally vital and alive for her in the moment or, alternatively, was only dutifully responding to my questions. And I was becoming increasingly aware of a feeling of pressure on my part to continually introduce new topics. As these feelings intensified, I decided that rather than continuing to pick up the slack, or to intentionally shift to a less active role (which I speculated might lead to a power struggle or an impasse), I would attempt to explore what was going on between us. So I began to metacommunicate with her—to engage her in the process of collaboratively exploring what was taking place between us by explicitly focusing on our relationship.

I thus said something to the effect of, "I find myself reflexively moving toward asking you more questions, in part I think as a way of keeping things going smoothly between us. But I'm also a bit concerned that if I continue doing this, it will get in the way of you talking about what feels most alive and important for you."

As I finished speaking, I felt Amanda tense up, and a sense of awkwardness began to emerge more clearly between us. She responded by saying, "I have no idea what you want me to talk about." I then made a number of attempts to explain what I was trying to get at and how exploring this further might be helpful. Rather than responding to my invitation to explore what was going on between us, however, it felt as if she was consistently trying to put the ball back in my court in an attempt to get me to take the lead again.

I considered the possibility of going back to asking for more factual information as a way of easing the tension but now felt at a loss for something to ask her. I was also beginning to feel that even if I could find more questions to ask Amanda, it would just be a way of going through the motions rather than talking about what was really happening, which is what seemed most meaningful to me at the moment. I began to get a sense of the two of us moving into an impasse. At the same time, experience has taught me that impasses of this type, although uncomfortable, are often part of an important emerging enactment that, if worked through constructively, can be a crucial part of the change process.

At this point, however, rather than risk alienating Amanda by trying to explore further, I attempted to strengthen the alliance by reiterating the rationale for my intervention (thereby increasing the possibility of collaboration on the therapeutic task). I attempted to explain to her that by exploring what was going on between us in the moment, we might be able to begin to shed some light on dynamics and relational patterns that were relevant to her current problems. She responded by saying, "I don't know what you're talking about. I don't understand."

I was aware of starting to feel inadequate, frustrated, and—to be frank—somewhat irritated. I found myself wondering if anything I said would be adequate for her right now. And I was beginning to wonder whether there was more to Amanda than was immediately apparent. At one level, I had begun to develop a sense of her as this sweet, fragile young woman who needed to be taken care of. Yet at the same time, I felt that she was putting me on the spot and that I was squirming. And as is often the case in these types of situations, I was not sure how much to trust my own countertransference feelings. To what extent were my growing feelings of inadequacy and irritation providing meaningful information about Amanda, and to what extent were my feelings simply "my problem"— something that I was bringing to the table?

At this point, in an attempt to clarify the connection between my attempts to explore what was going on between us and the problems that brought Amanda into treatment in the first place, I made the following interpretation: "It seems to me that one of the things you and I are struggling with right now in our relationship is the question of who is going to take the lead. I'm wondering in your relationships with men in general, who tends to take the lead?"

In response, she began to elaborate on a history of getting into relationships with domineering, abusive men who "take charge" in the relationship and whom she tended to "submit to." It emerged that she was used to following their lead rather than expressing her own needs and desires. Amanda described a need on her part to know what men want so that she would be able to provide it for them. She would then find herself submitting and feeling resentful. She also described a common pattern in her interactions with boyfriends in which initially she might explicitly disagree with them about something, but inevitably they would talk her into relinquishing her position and she would submit to them. And I began to wonder if there might be some element of this scenario being enacted in our relationship, in which my attempts to convince her of the value of exploring our relationship were fitting this template.

As the discussion continued, I began to speculate to myself about the nature of the enactment that might be playing out between us—I felt provoked by her but tried to maintain a sympathetic and understanding stance. Despite my best efforts to control my feelings of irritation and frustration, I worried that I would express my hostility indirectly and play the role of the perpetrator in a sadomasochistic enactment. To complicate things further, I was feeling badly about having negative feelings. I certainly don't like to think of myself as sadistic. And to be frank, knowing that we were being filmed, I was particularly concerned about coming across as cruel. In this context, my experience of internal conflict about my countertransference feelings was intensified by the unusual setting, but it is important to note that therapists often experience internal conflict about their countertransference feelings and that recognizing and working through these feelings of conflict are important parts of the therapist's internal work. For the time being, however, it felt as if we had returned to safer ground. I was asking questions about Amanda's relationships, she was responding cooperatively, and the feeling of tension between us had receded into the background.

Following a rather extensive and revealing discussion of Amanda's habitual pattern of getting into relationships with men who take the lead, as well as the price she pays for this, I attempted to make the link between this pattern and what was going on in our relationship. To my surprise, she denied seeing any connection between the two themes and did not acknowledge the possible value of exploring a potential connection. Furthermore, she continued to push me to explain the possible relevance of this type of exploration to her problems despite the fact that I had just struggled to do so. I again returned to my experience of feeling on the spot, inadequate, and speechless.

I responded with another attempt to provide Amanda with a rationale, and it once again fell on deaf ears; increasingly it seemed to me that any such attempts on my part would be futile. As the session came to an end, I attempted to reestablish some sense of collaboration with her by telling her that prior to the next session, l would think of how to explain things in a way that would be meaningful to her and encouraged her, in turn, to think about what we had been discussing and to reflect on whether she might be able to make sense of any part of what I had said or come up with any questions to ask me that might help clarify things for her.

Over the week between Sessions 2 and 3, I gave considerable thought to our session. At one level, it seemed likely that our current impasse was an enactment that was related in meaningful ways to a core theme in Amanda's problematic pattern in romantic relationships. On the other hand, part of me couldn't let go of the fantasy that if I could just come up with the right words, she would see what we were doing as meaningful and feel that I really was trying to help her. I considered the possibility of giving her various materials to read that would provide a more clear-cut rationale for the value of the type of exploration in which I was attempting to engage her.

And then I remembered the write-up that had been given to Amanda to read prior to her agreeing to participate in the project. At that point, I printed out a copy and read it. I was struck by the fact that it would be difficult for me to improve on what I had already written. "And this," I thought (feeling indignant and vindicated), "is the rationale that she had read and said made sense to her, before she agreed to participate in the project!" I toyed with the idea of actually reading it to her in the next session. Then it occurred to me that doing so might well be my way of continuing to play out the current enactment—a way of meanly proving to her that I was right and she was wrong.

Instead, I came up with a tentative plan for the next session of self-disclosing the nature of my internal processes between sessions as a way of leading into exploring and beginning to collaboratively make sense of the enactment that was taking place between us. I nevertheless put a copy of the rationale in my pocket so that I could refresh my memory just before the session, in case I ended up finding myself, once again, struggling to explain the purpose of the approach to her.

Toward the beginning of our third session, as a prelude to telling Amanda about my thinking between sessions, I asked her if she remembered the written statement she had read before starting our work together. To my surprise, she denied having ever seen the rationale. Now I was feeling completely stuck. I could try to explain it another time, but it was difficult for me to imagine any such attempt being more meaningful to her than it had been previously. Moreover, I anticipated that given my complicated feelings of anxiety, inadequacy, hopelessness about her being receptive, and irritation, it would be difficult for me to convey the rationale in a particularly articulate or compelling way. And then, in an act of desperation, I found myself reaching into my pocket to pull out a crumpled copy of the rationale. Perhaps I felt that reading from the written version that I had put considerable thought into composing would give me a greater sense of security and help me manage complex feelings that I anticipated were likely to undermine my ability to convey the rationale in an articulate and compelling way.

I began to read the rationale to Amanda, checking in with her periodically to see how she was reacting and whether things made sense to her. As this process continued, I began to experience a sense of confidence and mastery. Moreover, to my surprise, Amanda seemed to be engaging with me as I was reading and checking in with her. She was nodding, asking questions that I felt I could answer meaningfully, and apparently beginning to "get it."

At one level, I found myself skeptical that the rationale really made sense to her in a way that it hadn't in our previous session. I was essentially repeating what I had said before. Yet at the same time, I was sensing that something was beginning to shift in the dynamic of our relationship. In retrospect, I wonder if what really influenced the shift was not that I had conveyed new information to her but rather that my internal movement toward greater confidence and my assumption of a more authoritative, dominant stance allowed her to engage with me in a way that was more comfortable and familiar to her, that is, following the lead of a dominant male who was taking charge in the relationship. In retrospect, perhaps that was unconsciously part of my motivation for choosing to read the rationale in the first place—it was an attempt to regain some sense of mastery and control. Once I had finished reading, I felt that something was different, and I asked Amanda if the rationale made sense to her now. She responded, "Yes." And then after a short pause, she asked me, "But does it work?"

Amanda's stance was beginning to move from one of "I don't understand" to an articulation of an underlying skepticism and a desire for me to reassure her that I could help her. This allowed an opening for me to begin exploring her skepticism, a critical psychoanalytic process that can be conceptualized as a form of resistance analysis. As we continued to explore her underlying skepticism and she was able to experience me listening in an empathic and validating way, the alliance continued to strengthen.

After some exploration, I became concerned that to continue in this vein might feel too overwhelming to Amanda, especially given her previous reluctance to talk about our relationship and what was happening between the two of us in the here and now. I checked in with her to ask how she would like to proceed at this point (i.e., continue talking about her skepticism or move on to another topic). True to form, she responded, "What do you think?"—once again asking me to take the lead.

As in the previous session, I make an observation about the process between us (i.e., "It feels like I'm asking you to take the lead and you're asking me to take the lead"). Now however, something had shifted, and Amanda seemed more open to exploring the process. In response to my observation, she explained, "I turn to you because you're in charge here. You're the doctor." I was now struck by the fact that she was experiencing a vast power imbalance in our relationship. Although Amanda's perception of this power imbalance was completely understandable, until now it had been hard for me to fully grasp it at an experiential level, given that I had been feeling anything but authoritative in my relationship with her. This shift in my experience of Amanda in conjunction with her growing receptiveness allowed me an opening to explore further. In response to my exploration, she continued to open up. She spoke about not wanting to disappointment me and not wanting to "screw up" my "agenda." After all, she said, "We *are* here to produce a videotape."

And then it struck me that the same dynamic that tends to play out in many of Amanda's relationships—her pattern of trying to take care of the needs of the other person, submitting to their needs rather than asserting her own and then feeling resentful—might be playing out between the two of us as well. And although it might be tempting to simply see this as a form of transference on her part (i.e., a tendency to play out her typical patterns in the context of the therapeutic relationship), there was more to it than that. Her attempt to take care of my needs at the expense of her own was not taking place in a vacuum. Therapists always bring their own needs to the situation, whether it is the need for validation, the need for self-esteem, the need to help, or financial need. In this situation I had a pressing need to provide a good demonstration of my skills as a therapist. A clash in needs can be part of the underlying subtexts of any therapy and sometimes must be addressed explicitly and worked through.

My sense was that although Amanda was enacting a characteristic pattern of submitting to the needs of others, feeling resentful, and express-ing her resentment in a passive-aggressive fashion, she was also demonstrat-ing what I was coming to think of as a characteristic ability to read the subtlety of interpersonal situations and the courage to speak out and in a sense "talk about the elephant in the room." I was impressed by her perceptiveness and inner strength (which she has a tendency to disown), and I felt that it was important for me to validate her perceptions. Rather than commenting on her characteristic pattern of accommodating to others (an intervention that I was concerned she would experience as critical), I sensed it was more important to validate her perception and to highlight her disowned strengths. I thus acknowledged to Amanda that she was right that at least part of my agenda was selfish even if I was try-ing to help her. And I commended her on her ability to pick up on this. In retrospect, my impression is that my acknowledgment and acceptance of responsibility for my mixed agenda was another critical point in the positive shift in our alliance. The particular form of my mixed agenda (i.e., wanting to help vs. wanting to demonstrate a successful treatment for the video) was shaped by the context of the APA project in which we were both participating. It is important to point out, however, that as therapists we always have mixed agendas that are part of the context of the work, even if they are not talked about explicitly (I. Z. Hoffman, 1998; Slavin & Kriegman, 1998). The most obvious one is that we are there to help the client, and at the same time we are there to earn money.

In any event, Amanda seemed to appreciate my recognition of her perceptiveness, courage, and strength and my willingness to acknowledge my own conflicting agendas with her. And this paved the way for her to begin recognizing the way in which her tendency to look after my needs was preventing her from using this situation as an opportunity to meet some of her needs by making use of what I had to offer her. In the rest of this session, we continued to explore and work together in a much more collaborative fashion.

We developed a style of shifting seamlessly back and forth between focusing on Amanda's current life situation, her past, and our own relationship, and this helped to deepen the depth of exploration of her feelings, thoughts, and previously unarticulated experience in all three areas. From the very beginning of our work together, I had been struck by her sense of fragility, and subsequently I began to see a stronger side of her. As the sessions progressed and I came to experience an oscillation between the two of us in the roles of aggressor and victim, I developed a tentative formulation of Amanda as tending to dissociate her healthy aggression as part of her long-standing role of playing the caretaker and then needing to express her aggression indirectly or passive aggressively rather than through healthy self-assertion of her needs.

I continued to give Amanda feedback about my experience of these two different sides of her (i.e., strength vs. fragility), and she was intrigued and interested in exploring both sides. She acknowledged feeling pleased by my feedback about her strength and courage but also a little afraid, overwhelmed, and reluctant to fully take this feedback in. This led to an exploration of her fears of seeing and acknowledging her strengths as well as the defensive function of her fragile posture. If she were to fully accept her own strength and healthy aggression, without being able to retreat into her defensive posture of fragility, it would be too much responsibility for her to bear at that time. Rather than attempting to break through or do away with this aspect of her defensive style, I thus framed it in affirmative terms (i.e., it serves as kind of a safety net for her, and it's essential for her to hold on to that safety net as long as she needs it).

At one point in the context of exploring Amanda's tendency in her life to put other people's needs before her own (as she had been doing in our relationship), I asked her if she could remember how it had felt for her to play the role of the mediator between her mother and stepfather when she was a child. She recalled feeling a tremendous sense of responsibility, always having to make sure that things didn't get out of hand between the two of them. I empathized with the dread and pain that she must have experienced as well as the heavy burden. In response, she acknowledged that indeed it was only in the context of our work together that she was beginning to see how this whole experience must have (in her words) "screwed me up." At the same time, she said, she was also beginning to see that this developmental experience was part of where her current resources and strengths had come from. I responded something to the effect of, "Obviously there was a tremendous negative side to it, in that you were scared and had an overwhelming responsibility, but I imagine that the flip side is that it may have made you feel important, maybe even powerful."

This interpretation reflected an emerging semiarticulated formulation on my part of Amanda experiencing a type of secret narcissism and grandiosity. She responded, "I thought of that word but didn't want to say it." This led to an exploration of her fears of acknowledging her strengths and the dangers of not having the safety net of her stance as a victim to retreat to. Session 3 ended with Amanda expressing positive feelings about our work together and an impression on my part that a vitally important shift in the therapeutic alliance was beginning to take place.

In Sessions 4 and 5, our relationship continued to deepen, and Amanda gradually became more trusting and open. Among other things, she explored how difficult it had been in the past for her to trust and depend on other people, as well the ongoing impact of her need to take care of other people. As she spoke about both her fears of dependency and her fears about changing (an exploration of her resistance), the quality of her speech had a type of freshness and vitality that marked it as a genuine, emotionally immediate exploratory process. She then transitioned into speaking about her growing sense of trust or faith that things would work out for her and that she would be able to continue to change after the end of our work together. In general I was impressed by how engaged and animated she seemed in Sessions 4 and 5. In contrast to earlier sessions in which it felt like I had to work hard to generate questions to keep things going, Amanda seemed to be bringing herself to the session in a spontaneous and authentic way. During these sessions, she expressed a range of feelings, including sadness, hopelessness, and optimism about the future. Now there was no question on my part (as there had been, e.g., during Session 2) as to whether we were talking about things that felt affectively alive and meaningful to her. During these sessions, Amanda also showed more of the feisty and lively quality that I had begun to get a glimpse of in our first session, and our relationship was beginning to develop somewhat of a playful quality to it.

Session 6 (our final session) was a difficult but meaningful one. It had a tense, rough feeling to it not unlike some of our earlier sessions. Often, important themes reemerge around the time of termination, as both client and therapist deal with the realities of impending separation. I had a concern that, given Amanda's history of loss and the fact that she had begun to open up to me and trust me, she would experience the end of our work together as an abandonment.

I believe it is important to emphasize here that from a psychoanalytic perspective, Amanda would benefit from a longer term treatment in which she would have the opportunity to develop and sustain a trusting relationship with a therapist over a period of time. She could learn to trust someone and gradually modify her sense of implicit relational knowing or her internal object relations over time, through her experience of developing a relationship with a trustworthy and reliable therapist. A six-session treatment is extremely short for someone with her history, and I had been concerned that she would begin to open up and trust, only to be traumatized by a feeling of abandonment at the end.

All things considered, I believe it was a meaningful final session with moments of real engagement and connection between us in reviewing our time together. I remember feeling pressured and tense at the beginning of the session and wanting things to end on a good note. And I imagine Amanda may have had similar feelings. I normally consider it important to explore clients' feelings about termination and find that they are typically ambivalent. Clients are often reluctant to fully explore their disappointments. They can also be reluctant to fully explore their feelings when things go well. In these circumstances clients often have feelings of gratitude mixed with feelings of loss, abandonment, anxiety, and sometimes resentment about some of the things they did not get from their therapist.

In Amanda's case, however, I was particularly concerned about not wanting to pressure her to talk about feelings that might be difficult for her to fully experience, acknowledge, and express, especially given how difficult it had been for her to open up in the first place. I am thinking here of the dynamic that had emerged between us in the early stages of our work together, in which she would experience open-ended questions as difficult and invasive and respond by clamming up or putting the ball back in my court. I could easily imagine the same dynamic reemerging in our last session if I pushed too hard.

At the beginning of the session, I already sensed more reserve and cautiousness on Amanda's part than had been the case in the previous two sessions. And I, in turn, felt more cautious and more of a need to tread delicately. I began somewhat warily by asking her how she felt about this being our last session. In response, she acknowledged experiencing some ambivalent feelings: feelings that she would miss our sessions, combined with a sense of relief that she would no longer have to perform in front of a camera. I acknowledged having similar feelings as a way of helping to emphasize the mutual aspects of our relationship and of countering Amanda's tendency to feel powerless in our relationship and resentful because of this. By self-disclosing my own ambivalent feelings, I wanted to implicitly give her permission to speak more about her ambivalent feelings without putting any pressure on her to do so.

I asked Amanda if there was anything in particular that she wanted to talk about today, and she responded with an abrupt "Nope." Now I had a sense that if we were going to avoid getting into a power struggle, it would be important for me (at least at this juncture) to do more of the talking and to take more of the lead again. I told her that during our previous session, she had seemed to be "on a roll" and I had been reluctant to speak too much because she seemed very present and vitally alive, and I didn't want to interrupt her.

She responded that she didn't feel "on a roll" in this session. I told her that there were many things I wanted to ask her but that I felt cautious about not wanting to pressure her and put her on the spot. She seemed to relax with this disclosure, and then I told her that I felt curious about what she made of the time we had spent together, and whether there was anything in particular that stood out for her on reflection.

Amanda then told me that she was feeling a considerable difference between now and when we had first started. She felt that our time together had helped confirm her sense that she had made important changes in her life over the past year or so and that since we had started working together, she felt she had made even more progress. She was feeling more confident and more aware of her own strengths. She was feeling more trust in me, more trusting in general, and more hopeful about the future. She also said that she was beginning to have greater faith in herself and her ability to be more discriminating in her romantic choices.

I responded that what she was saying made perfect sense and that rationally I felt fine about us ending as well. I told her that, nevertheless, I felt sad ending our work together and concerned about not being able to be there for her in the future. My hope was that by disclosing this aspect of my experience, I would be giving her permission to contact any complementary feelings that she might have, even if she was not able to fully acknowledge or talk about them. At the end of the session, I gave Amanda some information about a local therapy clinic with a sliding scale. When the camera was turned off, the two of us walked over to the corner to briefly say goodbye. She spontaneously gave me a big hug, and I felt a sense of sadness and warmth toward her.

One year later, Amanda emailed me to let me know that she was doing well. She was still drug free and depression free, had gone into open-ended therapy with someone at the clinic to which I had referred her, and was finding the ongoing treatment helpful. She was also working full time and had begun a romantic relationship that sounded healthier than her previous romantic relationships.

In this chapter, I have discussed principles of intervention and underlying mechanisms of change in psychoanalytic treatment. I have also provided illustrations of change principles and the mechanisms through which they are hypothesized to operate in the context of both long-term and short-term psychoanalytic treatment.

# 5

# Evaluation

Many psychoanalysts are coming to realize that conducting research will be essential to the survival of psychoanalysis. Psychoanalysts have been slow to respond to the demand for empirically supported treatment and have often been dismissive of the efforts of psychoanalytically oriented investigators who do attempt to conduct this type of research. The well-documented gap between researchers and clinicians (Bergin & Strupp, 1973; Goldfried & Wolfe, 1996; Persons & Silberschatz, 1998; Rice & Greenberg, 1984; Safran, Greenberg, & Rice, 1988; Safran & Muran, 1994; Talley, Strupp, & Butler, 1994) that cuts across therapeutic orientations is particularly large in the psychoanalytic world. It is not unusual for psychoanalytic researchers to have no formal postgraduate psychoanalytic training and limited clinical practices.

The reasons for this are practical in part. It is extremely difficult to engage in the time-consuming activity of going through postgraduate

http://dx.doi.org/10.1037/0000190-005
*Psychoanalysis and Psychoanalytic Therapies, Second Edition*, by J. D. Safran and J. Hunter

psychoanalytic training while being a productive empirical researcher, making one's way up the formal ranks of academia in a university, and finding the time to successfully apply for the grant funding necessary to support good empirical research. And within the world of academic clinical psychology, psychoanalytically oriented researchers are fighting an uphill battle, as psychoanalysis becomes increasingly marginalized within the university system.

When it comes to government-supported research funding, the bias toward biological and neurophysiological research is making it increasingly difficult to receive funding for psychotherapy research in general. The common misconception that psychoanalytic therapy "lacks empirical support" makes it even more difficult to receive funding for psychoanalytically oriented research (I can testify to this on the basis of my experience serving on National Institute of Mental Health Grant review committees).

It is clear that the traditional psychoanalytic dismissiveness toward rigorous empirical research has been self-destructive and has had harmful effects on the development of the discipline. Although this attitude often reflects a narrow-minded dogmatism and insularity, it is also important to recognize that many psychoanalysts have valid concerns about the relevance to the practicing clinician of much of the psychotherapy research that is published. There are well-founded concerns about the limits of existing research paradigms and their abilities to capture the complexity of the therapeutic process.

## THE NEED FOR RANDOMIZED CLINICAL TRIALS

The gold standard for psychotherapy research is the randomized clinical trial (RCT), which was borrowed from medication research that assumes that it is possible to evaluate the efficacy of a particular medication independent of the interpersonal context in which it is delivered. In this framework, the medication is the "active ingredient," and all the other elements that may have an impact on its efficacy (e.g., client expectations, therapist interpersonal skill, quality of the therapeutic relationship) are extraneous, nonspecific factors that can be controlled for. The problem with applying this "drug metaphor" (Stiles & Shapiro, 1989) to psychosocial treatments is that in psychotherapy, any active ingredient of the treatment is conceptually inseparable from the so-called nonspecific factors (e.g., the emergent properties of the client–therapist relationship). It is thus conceptually impossible to separate out the therapy from the therapist (or more accurately, the therapeutic dyad). In fact, a large and growing body of evidence indicates that factors such as the therapeutic relationship and the individual therapist variable contribute considerably more to the outcome variance than the particular brand of psychotherapy being practiced (Safran, 2003; Safran & Muran, 2000; Safran & Segal, 1990; Wampold, 2001).

It is clear that it is vital to conduct RCT research on psychoanalytically oriented treatment for the purposes of influencing public attitudes and the attitudes of policymakers (both government and private insurance companies). Some of the most important empirical results are detailed next. However, it is important to carefully consider the rigorous and thoughtful critiques of those who argue that there are dangers of wholeheartedly embracing the enterprise of documenting the value of psychoanalytically oriented treatments through RCTs (e.g., Cushman & Gilford, 2000; I. Z. Hoffman, 2009). As I indicated earlier, Cushman and Gilford (2000) argued that some of the implicit assumptions underlying the evidenced-based treatment paradigm (e.g., speed, concreteness, efficiency, systematization) can have a harmful impact on the way we understand the therapeutic process. They argued that this paradigm conceptualizes the therapist as a type of psychotechnician who delivers a standardized technique in a maximally efficient fashion. This lends itself implicitly to a view of the client as a passive recipient of this technique who varies in terms of the extent that he or she is compliant with the treatment protocol. Along similar lines, I. Z. Hoffman (2009) argued that the problem with overemphasizing the importance of demonstrating the "scientific validity" of the psychoanalytic enterprise is that valid critiques of the relevant underlying philosophical and epistemological assumptions can become marginalized. According to Hoffman, the evaluation of manual-based treatments ignores the uniqueness of each therapeutic dyad and the intrinsic indeterminacy of the therapeutic process. Moreover, from his perspective, making the claim that one can know what will be most helpful for a particular client on the basis of empirical evidence is a form of technical rationality that masks the therapist's personal responsibility for making value-based choices as to how to respond in any given moment. Finally, our assumptions about what constitutes treatment effectiveness implicitly involve value judgments about how to define healthy functioning. Such questions cannot and should not be adjudicated entirely by "science." To the extent that we give the authority of science the power to arbitrate these choices, we are falling into the worst kind of scientism, in which moral positions masquerade as scientific "findings" (I. Z. Hoffman, 2009, p. 1049).

My own perspective is that the efforts of psychoanalytically oriented researchers are vital to the survival of psychoanalysis. The failure to conduct RCT research on psychoanalytically oriented treatments allows for the perpetuation of the distorted perception that psychoanalytic treatment does not have empirical support. People want straightforward concrete answers about "what works," and they have little time or inclination to follow what can seem like esoteric debates among professionals.

## RESEARCH SUPPORTING THE EFFECTIVENESS OF PSYCHOANALYSIS AND PSYCHOANALYTIC THERAPY

In an influential *American Psychologist* article, Shedler (2010) reviewed the results of eight meta-analyses of studies evaluating the efficacy of psychodynamic therapy. The studies in these meta-analyses included only well-designed RCTs comparing psychoanalytically oriented treatments with a range of different control conditions, including cognitive and behavioral treatments. Client populations in these studies included adults presenting with a range of disorders including depression, anxiety, panic, somatoform disorders, eating disorders, substance-related disorders, and personality disorders. The majority of the psychodynamic treatments included in these studies were short term in nature (which is typically the case for RCTs). The meta-analyses reviewed found substantial effects for psychodynamic treatments, with effective outcomes as large as or larger than those commonly found for cognitive and behavioral treatments. In addition, the results indicate that clients who receive psychodynamic therapy maintain therapeutic gains and appear to continue to improve after treatment ends.

More recently, the research team of Leichsenring extensively reviewed RCTs of psychodynamic psychotherapy. They found that psychodynamic psychotherapy is effective for a variety of diagnoses, including anxiety and depression (Leichsenring, Klein, & Salzer, 2014; Leichsenring, Luyten, et al., 2015). Moreover, this was the case when applying the criteria employed by the Task Force on Promotion and Dissemination of Psychological Procedures to identify effective treatments (Chambless & Hollon, 1998; Leichsenring, Leweke, Klein, & Steinert, 2015), meaning that the psychodynamic treatment earned the designation of "empirically validated." Abbass et al. (2014) obtained similar results using the Cochrane Database, which was set up as an independent source of evidence to inform health care decisions.

Recent rigorous meta-analyses supported these conclusions as well and found that psychodynamic psychotherapy was superior to control treatments and just as effective as alternative treatments (Driessen et al., 2015; Keefe, McCarthy, Dinger, Zilcha-Mano, & Barber, 2014; Kivlighan et al., 2015). Moreover, the effects lasted just as long for psychodynamic treatment as for alternative treatments (Kivlighan et al., 2015).

Barber, Muran, McCarthy, and Keefe (2013, in press) presented a comprehensive and very nuanced discussion of the meta-analyses of dynamic therapies for (a) mood, (b) anxiety, and (c) personality disorders, then reviewed the literature on dynamic change processes and mechanisms, such as insight, defenses, rigidity, object relations, reflective functioning, and therapeutic alliance (including rupture-repair). In regard to personality disorders, Barber et al. (in press) concluded, "Unambiguously, DTs [dynamic therapies] should be considered viable and efficacious treatments for personality pathology." This chapter and the Norcross and Lambert (2018) article go beyond looking at outcome and are able to provide meta-analytic reviews of such dynamically informed relationship variables as the alliance, rupture-repair, and countertransference.

In addition to the studies included in these meta-analyses, recent studies provided evidence that psychoanalytically oriented treatments can be effective in the treatment of borderline personality disorder and challenged the conventional wisdom that dialectical behavior therapy (DBT) is the only treatment of choice for this population. In the first study involving a head-to-head competition between DBT and a psycho-analytically oriented treatment that makes extensive use of transference interpretations, Clarkin, Levy, Lenzenweger, and Kernberg (2007) randomly assigned borderline clients to either DBT or the psycho-analytically oriented treatment and found the analytically oriented treat-ment to be as effective as or more effective than DBT. Finally, they found that clients in the analytically oriented treatment were significantly more likely than DBT clients to change their attachment status from the insecure to the secure category as assessed by the Adult Attachment Interview.

Bateman and Fonagy (2008) evaluated the effectiveness of a psycho-analytic treatment that they developed, designated as *mentalization-based treatment*, which is designed as an intervention for clients with border-line personality disorder. Their research demonstrated that with this population, mentalization-based treatment is significantly more effective than treatment as usual (partial hospitalization) on a range of outcome measures at both termination and at an 18-month follow-up. In a longer term follow-up study with the same sample, Bateman and Fonagy (2008) found that 5 years after discharge, the clients treated psychoanalytically continued to show statistical superiority to treatment-as-usual clients on a number of important dimensions, including suicidality (23% vs. 74%), service use (2.0 years vs. 3.5 years of psychiatric outpatient treatment), use of medication, global function above 60 (45% vs. 10%), vocational status (employed or in education 3.2 years vs. 1.2 years), and diagnostic status (13% vs. 87% continued to meet diagnostic criteria for borderline personality disorder).

Finally, McMain et al. (2009) evaluated the efficacy of DBT combined with medication relative to psychodynamically informed treatment combined with medication for clients diagnosed with borderline personality disorder. Treatment length in both conditions was 1 year. This was the largest RCT that included DBT as a treatment modality to date. Counter to McMain et al.'s expectation, both treatment groups showed significant improvement across a range of outcome measures at termination, and there was no significant difference between the two groups. Although there is nothing dramatic about findings that fail to find a significant difference, these findings are surprising given the widely acknowledged *researcher allegiance effect* in psychotherapy research (i.e., the finding that the theoretical allegiance of the researcher is the most powerful predictor of treatment outcome; Luborsky et al., 1999) and the fact that McMain is a DBT proponent.

Certain practical and logistical problems make it extremely difficult to conduct RCTs of long-term intensive treatments of any type, including psychoanalysis. One practical problem is that tracking the progress of clients over a significant length of time in treatment (4–6 years or more) requires a significant investment of time and resources. In addition, it is extremely difficult to find clients who are willing to be randomly assigned to one of two treatments that differ radically with respect to both treatment duration and intensity. Because of these constraints, many studies evaluating the effectiveness of long-term psychoanalysis tend to be of a more naturalistic nature (e.g., clients either self-select their treatments or are assigned to the treatment condition on the basis of assessed suitability) and are thus subject to various methodological problems. The majority of the research on the effectiveness of medium to long-term psychoanalytic and psychoanalytically oriented treatment is conducted in European countries in which the public health care system covers the cost of long-term psychoanalytically oriented treatment. For example, in Germany, Leichsenring, Biskup, Kreische, and Staats (2005) reported the results of a naturalistic study of the effectiveness of psychoanalytic therapy for 36 clients seeking treatment for chronic psychological problems (e.g., depression, anxiety, obsessive-compulsive disorder, and nonorganic sexual dysfunction), with the majority of clients presenting with comorbid diagnostic pictures. Although there was no control group, the effect size of a control group from another study was used as a point of reference. The average duration of treatment was 37.4 months, and on average, 253 sessions were conducted. In general, improvement was found for symptoms, interpersonal problems, quality of life, and the target problem formulated by the clients themselves at the beginning of treatment. These changes were stable at 1-year follow-up, and in some areas they actually increased.

An extremely ambitious naturalistic outcome study conducted in Sweden by Sandell et al. (2000) evaluated outcome for more than 400 clients who received either psychoanalysis or psychoanalytically oriented psychotherapy. The mean duration of treatment in psychoanalysis was 51 months, and the mean frequency was 3.5 sessions per week. The mean length of treatment in psychotherapy was 40 months, and the mean frequency of sessions was 1.4 times per week. In general both treatments were found be effective, but (a) at the 3-year follow-up interval clients in psychoanalysis achieved a better outcome on a number of dimensions than clients in psychotherapy, and (b) more experienced psychoanalysts achieved a better outcome than therapists with less psychoanalytic training and experience.

An important study by Huber, Henrich, Gastner, and Klug (2012) used a partially randomized, quasi-experimental design to evaluate differences in the effectiveness for depressed patients of intensive psychoanalytic treatment (average duration was between 160 and 240 sessions; session frequency were two to three sessions per week), less intensive psychodynamic treatment (average duration was 50–80 sessions; session frequency was one time per week), and cognitive behavior therapy (average duration was between 45 and 60 sessions; session frequency was one time per week). At termination, significantly more clients in the psychoanalytic group (91%) than clients in the cognitive behavior therapy condition (53%) no longer met diagnostic criteria for depression. Patients in the less intensive psychodynamic condition fell in between, with 68% no longer meeting criteria for depression.

At 1-year follow-up, 89% of the psychoanalytic clients, 68% of the psychodynamic clients, and 42% of the cognitive-behavioral clients no longer met diagnostic criteria for depression. The differences were significant between psychoanalytic and cognitive behavior therapies, between psychoanalytic and psychodynamic therapies, and between psychodynamic and cognitive behavior therapies. The findings indicating significant differences between psychodynamic and cognitive-behavioral conditions at follow-up were striking, given the fact that the two treatments were provided at approximately the same duration and intensity.

Finally, there are extensive reviews of a large number of naturalistic studies investigating the effectiveness of intensive, long-term psychoanalytic treatments (e.g., Fonagy et al., 1999; Galatzer-Levy, Bachrach, Skolnikoff, & Waldron, 2000; Richardson, Kachele, & Renlund, 2004). In general, the results are quite promising.

In summary, a growing body of empirical evidence supports the efficacy of psychoanalytically oriented interventions for a range of disorders. Moreover, an emerging body of evidence suggests that the impact of psychoanalytically oriented interventions continues to increase after termination (a finding that is not emerging to the same extent in the case of cognitive-behavioral interventions). At this point in time, for practical and logistical reasons, the evidence for the effectiveness of intensive long-term psychoanalysis is garnered from naturalistic studies rather than RCTs.

It would be a mistake, however, to ignore the findings of the many naturalistic studies supporting the effectiveness of long-term psychoanalysis. In fact, as many have argued (e.g., Seligman, 1995; Westen, Novotny, & Thompson-Brenner, 2004), naturalistic studies (despite their limitations) have certain advantages over RCTs with respect to external validity and generalizability. Unlike subjects in RCTs, in real life clients choose the type of therapy they are receiving, as well as their therapists, and they remain in treatment until they decide that it is time to terminate. Moreover, therapists as a rule do not adhere to standardized rigid protocols and are more likely to modify what they are doing in response to the client's needs in any given session and over time. Empirical research inevitably purchases internal validity (the ability to infer causation and rule out alternative hypotheses) at the expense of external validity (generalizability to real-life situations). If the yield of psychotherapy research is to be of any real value, it is essential for us to adopt a pluralistic perspective that weighs the evidence produced by a range of different methodologies in light of an understanding of the strengths and weaknesses of any given methodology (Safran, 2001).

# 6

# Future Developments

Much ink has been spilt over the years on the topic of whether psychoanalysis has a future. I start this section with the assumption that psychoanalysis does indeed have a future and that this future will come in a variety of shapes and forms. One form will involve the ongoing integration of psychoanalytic ideas into other forms of treatment, especially cognitive therapy. In the early to mid-1990s, I published a number of articles and books with collaborators, advocating for the use of psychoanalytic conceptualizations of the therapeutic relationship within cognitive therapy. I argued that these conceptualizations could facilitate the assessment and formulation process, help to work through therapeutic impasses, increase treatment maintenance, and enrich our understanding of the relationship between emotion and cognition (Greenberg & Safran, 1987; Safran, 1984, 1998; Safran & Greenberg, 1991; Safran & Segal, 1990). Contemporary cognitive therapy now includes

http://dx.doi.org/10.1037/0000190-006
*Psychoanalysis and Psychoanalytic Therapies, Second Edition*, by J. D. Safran and J. Hunter

features that were once considered irrelevant, including exploring the therapeutic relationship, using the therapeutic relationship as a vehicle of change, helping clients to become aware of feelings they are avoiding, exploring the client's past, and extending the length of treatment.

Another form will be the extension of psychoanalysis as it reconciles to the realities of current practice and integrates techniques from other traditions to flexibly meet clients' needs. I believe that psychoanalysis will continue to survive as a distinct tradition but that to flourish and maintain its vitality, it will have to continue to evolve. There is a discrepancy between the psychoanalysis that candidates in traditional institutes are trained to conduct and value and contemporary practice. The psychoanalysis of the future will need to continue to abandon the elitist emphasis on ideological purity and come in a range of different forms, treatment lengths, and intensities. Psychoanalytic training institutes will also need to broaden their curricula to offer training in a variety of important areas that are not commonly covered, including brief-term therapy; integrating psychoanalysis with other treatment modalities; working with intersectional identities; marital, family, and group therapy; and working with specific populations such as trauma victims and severe personality disorders. Many curriculum changes of this type are already taking place, especially within the more innovative, nontraditional psychoanalytic institutes. But it will be important for changes like this to become more widespread.

## PRACTICAL PSYCHOANALYSIS

In a culture in which psychoanalysis has come to be associated with a form of indulgent self-preoccupation for the idle and financially comfortable elite, the term *practical psychoanalysis* seems like an oxymoron. There is no doubt that psychoanalysis values deep changes in personality structure and relational dynamics. At the same time, there is a growing realization among psychoanalysts that the reluctance to focus on client symptoms and to concern themselves with relief can represent a failure to take clients' suffering seriously and to provide them with the type of help they are seeking. Owen Renik (2006) made the following argument:

People who seek the help of mental health caregivers want a therapy that will provide maximum relief from emotional distress as quickly as possible. Most clinical psychoanalysts offer instead a lengthy journey of self-discovery during which too much concern with symptom relief is considered counterproductive. "Self-awareness" is the main goal; symptom relief is of secondary importance and is expected to arrive, if at all, only after a while. (p. 1)

From Renik's (2006) perspective, this type of stance is unfortunate because it all too often fails to provide clients with relief for the suffering that brings them to treatment in the first place. Although a psychoanalytic therapist may be able convince a client that the project of self-discovery is worthwhile, there is always a danger that the client will stay in therapy as a form of compliance even if client's symptoms are not addressed or leave treatment because he or she doesn't find it to be of any value.

Renik (2006) thus argued for the importance of collaborating with clients in the ongoing process of establishing shared treatment goals. When the therapist has a different perspective on these issues than the client, Renik argued that it is important for the therapist to be explicit about these differences to give the client an opportunity to take another perspective into consideration and decide whether he or she wishes to be influenced by it. From Renik's perspective, this type of candidness, far from using the therapist's authority to unduly influence the client (a traditional concern for psychoanalysts), actually "levels the playing field" by letting the client know explicitly where the therapist is coming from so that he or she does not end up being manipulated by a hidden agenda. He also encouraged therapists to engage in an ongoing process of explicitly exploring with the client the extent to which he or she feels that the treatment is beneficial

Many other analysts over the years (e.g., Bader, 1994; Connors, 2006; Frank, 1999; Wachtel, 1977, 1997) have argued for the importance of taking the client's symptoms seriously and using a range of more active interventions to help the client obtain symptom relief. An emphasis on the client's symptoms does not have to neglect the underlying meaning of these symptoms or the interpersonal context in which they are embedded.

Moreover, experiencing symptom relief may pave the way for the client to begin to explore other issues of a deeper nature.

Many years ago while working in a psychiatric hospital, I supervised a young trainee in the use of behavioral interventions to treat a client presenting with a needle phobia that prevented her from seeking any medical treatment because of the threat of receiving an injection. Although the behavioral treatment was apparently successful, a year later the client returned to a different clinic in the same hospital to seek treatment. She was referred back to our clinic for an assessment, and I met with her. It turned out that she had indeed been helped by her treatment with us and was no longer troubled by the same presenting problem. Now, however, she said that she was ready to work on some interpersonal concerns that, in her words, she "hadn't been thinking about so much" at the time she had initially been treated in our clinic. In recounting this case, I want to be clear that I am not rehashing the old psychoanalytic argument that treating the symptom is pointless because it is a manifestation of a deeper underlying problem, which will ultimately result in the emergence of a new symptom. Quite the contrary, I am arguing for the importance of "meeting clients where they are." If we had attempted initially to treat this client with an insight-oriented approach, she may well have dropped out of treatment. Instead, perhaps the process of engaging her at the level that was meaningful to her helped her begin to develop the sense of trust and safety to subsequently pursue deeper, more threatening psychological issues.

## INTEGRATING APPROACHES

As part of the flexibility required to meet all of the complex goals of psychotherapy, many psychoanalysts have advocated for integrating interventions from other therapeutic perspectives into psychoanalytic practice. In *The Handbook of Psychotherapy Integration*, Norcross and Goldfried (2019) pointed out that integrating techniques from different clinical approaches is now the norm for practitioners and no longer the exception. Numerous models for how psychotherapy integration can take place have been proposed; the most relevant is assimilative integration. Assimilative integration is a mode of conducting psychotherapy in which a technique, concept, or perspective is incorporated into one's preferred therapeutic approach (Messer, 2015). For example, an analyst could practice a relaxation exercise in session. This stands in contrast to eclecticism, in that the clinician still primarily identifies with one "home" orientation.

Consistent with the movement away from orthodoxy that has taken place in psychoanalysis over the past 40 years, analysts have looked toward other practices in order to have more technical flexibility and choice. Wachtel (1977, 1997, 2011, 2014) was an early advocate of the potential usefulness of incorporating behavioral interventions and systemic understanding into psychoanalytic practice, arguing in his theory of cyclical psychodynamics that such interventions can actually facilitate changes at a psychodynamic level and that psychoanalytic theory could add a valuable dimension to understanding factors causing and maintaining problems that are manifested at a behavioral level.

Frank (1999) has written extensively about the way in which the relational turn in psychoanalysis (i.e., the emergence of relational psychoanalysis) provides a theoretical framework that is compatible with the use of active behavioral interventions by psychoanalytically oriented therapists and with more contemporary theoretical developments in psychoanalysis, and he has provided illuminating clinical examples illustrating the potential fruitfulness of integrating psychoanalytic and behavioral approaches. Bresler and Starr (2015) provided us with a highly informative collection of examples of relational analysts incorporating techniques and perspectives from other traditions. These include cognitive behavior therapy, Zen Buddhism, dialectical behavior therapy, neurofeedback, and body-focused therapeutic techniques.

It is important to keep in mind that if an analyst uses a behavioral technique, for example, he would do so while retaining a psychodynamic perspective. An analyst will always be considering the deeper meaning behind all activity in the treatment, including his or her own choices. He will be considering the meaning of the active intervention in light of the client's personal history and dynamics and will be sensitive to the transference implications. The use of a technique introduced by the analyst will inevitably be part of an enactment in the treatment dyad that needs to be understood on an ongoing basis. For example, the introduction of a relaxation exercise in session could reflect the analyst's discomfort with the client's affective experience and could unwittingly cause the client to be more circumspect about sharing certain feelings. Conversely, it could elicit a regressive dependence in a client, which the analyst might experience as making him feel more powerful. These interlocking dynamics would have to be understood in the same way that all other interpersonal enactments are. Gold and Stricker (2015) argued, interestingly, that not using a helpful technique could also be understood as an enactment within the treatment, with the analyst taking on the role of a passive, neglectful, or helpless parent. They suggested some active interventions that can comfortably be assimilated into a dynamic treatment, including social skills training and the assignment of homework.

## PSYCHOANALYTIC TREATMENTS AND SOCIOCULTURAL IDENTITIES

Psychoanalysis was originally developed as a form of treatment by and for educated middle-class Western Europeans, yet the principles were regarded as universal to all people, irrespective of culture or class. As psychoanalysis became the dominant theoretical influence within the public health care system in the United States, a paradoxical process took place. Therapists influenced by psychoanalytic thinking were placed in the position of treating a broad range of clients from different cultures and social classes. At the same time, they were being guided by theoretical premises and intervention principles ill-equipped to fit the diversity of clients being treated. In recent years, as the field has become more diverse and democratic, psychoanalysts have written extensively about the importance of recognizing middle-class Euro-American biases of psychoanalytic theory and practice. They have also written extensively about the importance of modifying theory, clinical stance, and interventions in a fashion that incorporates an understanding of the cultural attitudes, assumptions, and structural social ramifications salient to a full range of different cultures and social classes (see, e.g., Altman, 2010; Gentile, 2013; Gutwill & Hollander, 2006; Leary, 2000; Padrón, 2019; Perez Foster, Moskowitz, & Javier, 1996; Pogue White, 2002; Saketopoulou, 2011; Tummala-Narra, 2016; Yi, 2014). The discussion of themes such as individualism/collectivism, social hierarchy and respect for authority, gender roles, spirituality, and cultural difference in emotional expression has been afforded greater primacy in contemporary psychoanalytic thinking after having been neglected by the field for many years.

What psychoanalysis can uniquely contribute to questions concerning the relationship between mind and culture is its recognition of unconscious material, including biases and prejudices, about race, culture, and class and how these shape our daily interactions. We inevitably internalize societal prejudices, and these unconscious internalized attitudes influence the way in which we relate to others and to ourselves. Internalized attitudes about culture and race play out unconsciously in the transference/countertransference matrix for both client and therapist (Akhtar, 2006; Altman, 2000; Leary, 2000; Pogue White, 2002). Neil Altman (2000) wrote a candid article about a treatment with an African American client: Together they became embroiled in a social and relational process that Leary (2000) called *racial enactment*. Racial enactments are interpersonal sequences shaped by unconscious attitudes regarding race (Leary, 2000). In this case, Altman, a middle-class Jewish American psychoanalyst, treated an African American client, whom he called Mr. A, for marital problems and panic attacks. Altman initially found himself feeling tremendously admiring of Mr. A for having achieved so much even though the deck was stacked against him. Early in treatment, however, a pattern began to emerge in which Mr. A would miss appointments with Altman and bounce checks. Although Altman attempted to address the situation with Mr. A, he failed to explore the potential meaning of what was taking place between them as fully as he might with another client. In retrospect, Altman recognized that even before the first check had bounced, a marginal thought had occurred to him that Mr. A might end up not paying him. In Altman's words, the thought went something like, "I can't believe that this man, who has fought his way up from poverty and who still struggles to make ends meet, is going to give substantial sums of money to a privileged person like me." At a somewhat deeper level, Altman admits to having the racially prejudiced thought that Mr. A might stiff him because he was Black and because of Altman's own semiconscious racist stereotypes involving "Black people, irresponsibility, and criminality" (p. 594), together with a self-referring, complementary, and shame-inducing anti-Jewish stereotype surrounding greed. In retrospect, Altman speculated that his own feelings of shame about his semiconscious racist feelings and his internalized anti-Semitism prevented him from exploring the situation as constructively as he might have with Mr. A. Although there is no way of knowing if a deeper exploration of the potentially unconscious racial undertones to the enactment might have been beneficial for the treatment, I believe that Altman has provided a valuable example of the way in which semiconscious or unconscious race-related attitudes can potentially play out in a transference/countertransference enactment.

Moving beyond the scope of the previous example, there is a growing trend within certain pockets of the psychoanalytic community to use an intersectional approach in their case conceptualization and practice. *Intersectionality*, a term coined by the Black feminist scholar Kimberlé Crenshaw in the twilight of the 1980s, refers to a way of understanding people, their identities, and their social standing within society. It holds that social categories—such as race, gender, sexual orientation, and class—weave together to determine a person's standing within a social hierarchy and shape their experience of themselves in relation to others in a society that privileges some identities at the expense of others (Crenshaw, 2020). Although psychoanalysis has often neglected struc-tural social and identity-related factors in thinking about the relationship between patient and clinician, there has been a recent change toward an intersectional perspective. This turn toward the impact of social reality on the treatment frame has focused, particularly, on how intersecting identities and the sociopolitical positions of the patient and clinician shape the transference/countertransference matrix and treatment (Gentile, 2013; Padrón, 2019; Saketopoulou, 2011; Tummala-Narra, 2016; Yi, 2014; Young-Bruehl, 2006).

To illuminate how this approach works, Gentile (2013) wrote about how a psychoanalytic psychotherapy might be complicated by the uneven distribution of power and privilege within social and cultural reality. She explored how her intersecting identities, as a White female psychotherapist, interact with the interleaving identities of a female Latina patient reckoning with complex sexual trauma (Gentile, 2013). Gentile articulated the dilemmas of identification shaping the patient–therapist relationship, paying close attention to how broader structural social factors constrain the expression and reception of empathy within the dyad. She articulated the link between relational dynamics and sociocultural contingencies and how the respective social positions of patient and clinician influence the potential for closeness, support, identification, and healing within the therapeutic dyad.

To illustrate, Gentile (2013) described the case of an anxious 23-year-old Latina psychology student she called Vasialys. Vasialys lived with her mother, two teenage brothers, and an 8-year-old sister, and she entered treatment before her father was about to be released from jail after serving 8 months for driving on a suspended license. She presented with dissociated trauma linked to her father's physical and verbal abuse of both her and her mother. Her father had sexually abused her when she was between the ages of 6 and 10, a violence she spoke of as if it no longer impacted her. Gentile wrote that she narrated her trauma in a flat, low, and disconnected tone, noting that "she did not have a verbal language to describe what had happened" (p. 460). Much of the treatment involved working through Vasialys's feeling of responsibility for the abuse she suffered, toward being able to identify her father as an aggressor who abused her. Here, Gentile illuminated, from an intersectional vantage point, the vexed relational possibilities for identification existing between them that threatened to toxify the empathy expressed by Gentile toward Vasialys.

Gentile (2013) drew attention to how an intersectional outlook requires that clinicians reflect deeply on their own subjectivity, their social standing, and its complementary structural culpability. She acknowledged with refreshing frankness her own struggle, as a White clinician in the United States, in finding adequate empathic therapeutic pathways that did not automatically deem Vasialys's Latina identity guilty for the transgressions of her father. Gentile recognized that to move forward in the treatment—to cocreate a language with Vasialys that would allow her to discover her own agency—she needed to acknowledge and analyze her own intersecting identities and social standing beyond the walls of her office. Gentile stressed the cultural bind in which Vasialys, as a Latina, found herself unconsciously mired: To acknowledge the violence wrought on her by her father, a Latino, with a White clinician, she had to implicate her cultural identity "in yet another violent crime, when the dominant culture already casts Latinos primarily as criminals" (p. 463). To unequivocally receive Gentile's support, empathy, and solidarity, Vasialys had to accuse Latino culture.

Whereas Gentile demonstrated what an intersectional approach has to offer psychoanalysis, Carlos Padrón, with roots in Venezuela, articulated what the process of psychoanalysis has to offer patients struggling with identity-related psychic suffering. In Padrón's vision of the therapeutic action of psychoanalytic process, the emergent interaction between patient and clinician creates space for the exploration and transformation of the dynamic interaction between the sociopolitical, historical, and cultural forces that constitute the patient's identity. This affords the patient the freedom to move beyond a reified self-understanding in order to "imagine [themselves] otherwise" (Padrón, 2019, p. 190). Both Gentile and Padrón are committed to, to borrow the words of Pratyusha Tummala-Narra (2016), "bringing social context into the foreground of psychoanalysis" to help patients contend with the depth and complexity of their inter- and intrapsychic conflicts and experience. Although some psychoanalytic clinicians and scholars may shy away from an intersectional approach because of the complex and entangled nature of our social identities, it becomes ever more vital to embrace as psychotherapy contends with a rapidly changing and globalizing society.

As I have discussed throughout the book, a contemporary psychoanalytic perspective emphasizes the role of a host of change mechanisms, including relational, sociopolitical, and cultural experience; containment; and affective communication and regulation. Intersectional psycho-analytic approaches recognize the role of sociological, political, and cultural forces that form patients' identities and experiences of themselves operating within an unequal society. To echo Padrón (2019), who harkened back to the subversive origins of psychoanalytic thinking, the psychoanalytic process facilitates the exploration, insight gain, and working-through of the dynamic interaction between a patient's conscious and unconscious psychic activity and their social, political, and cultural realities.

## SOCIAL, CULTURAL, AND POLITICAL CRITIQUE

Psychoanalysis has not always been a progressive force in society. For example, in the mid-20th century, mainstream analysts endorsed a con-servative heteronormative definition of mental health, which pathologized people with other sexual orientations (Drescher 2008). However, over recent decades analysts have begun to reclaim a subversive, critical perspec-tive on societal issues. Psychoanalytic thinking can be fruitful in helping us understand everything from the fantasies that underly the election of certain leaders to the denial of annihilation, which disables us from acting decisively on climate change. From Botticelli's (2004) perspective, "We need to take ourselves more seriously and to hold onto the strength of our relational convictions after we leave our offices" (p. 649). He argued that it is imperative for clinicians not to divorce the psychological from the political or to retreat exclusively to the psychological realm, as a defensive reaction to hopelessness and our fears that actions in the political realm will prove futile.

Nancy Caro Hollander, a professor of Latin American history and a psychoanalyst, has written about the role that politically engaged psycho-analysts played in the fight for human rights under Latin American military regimes during the 1970s and 1980s (e.g., Hollander, 1997, 2006, 2010). In her book *Love in a Time of Hate*, Hollander (1997) documented the experiences of a number of politically active psychoanalysts from Argen-tina, Uruguay, and Chile who found ways of struggling for democracy and human rights under dictatorships in their countries. Some of them were imprisoned and tortured by the military governments, and others escaped to countries such as Mexico, Cuba, and France.

Hollander (2006, 2010) has pointed out parallels between the situation in Latin America and in the United States right now. With the growing infringement of American civil liberties, following the attacks on the World Trade Center, Hollander urged her colleagues in the United States to learn from the experience of Latin American psychoanalysts who had lived through the experience of their countries' slow drift from democratic to totalitarian forms of government. She also warned against the dangers potentially resulting from mental health professionals dissociating the psychological from the political.

In recent years, psychoanalysts in the United States have been connecting the psychological and the political and have taken action. Following the invasion of Afghanistan, the American government made a decision to engage in coercive interrogation practices that violate the protections guaranteed by the Geneva Convention regarding detainees in detention sites such as Abu Ghraib and Guantánamo Bay. A series of articles in *The New York Times*, and elsewhere, alleged that professionals and other health professionals were playing an integral role in devising and consulting on abusive interrogation techniques at Guantánamo that were "tantamount to torture." The International Committee of the Red Cross (ICRC) described this as "a flagrant violation of professional ethics" (Lewis, 2004). Congressional investigations revealed that psychologists had designed and helped to implement torture programs for the Department of Defense at Guantánamo and for the CIA at various "black sites" around the world.

In response, many psychologists urged the American Psychological Association (APA) to establish policy that would explicitly prohibit psychologists from working at certain military sites. Among the leaders of this effort were members of APA's Division of Psychoanalysis (39), including Neil Altman, Ghislaine Boulanger, Ruth Fallenbaum, Steven Reisner, Stephen Soldz and Frank Summers. Although APA's (2017) ethics code prohibited violations of human rights, the involvement of military psychologists in enhanced interrogation of detainees was the subject of controversy, and activist psychologists who felt that any such participation was a violation of human rights and should be banned brought a referendum before the entire APA membership. The aim of the referendum was to prohibit psychologists from working "in settings where persons are held outside of, or in violation of, either International Law or the U.S. Constitution unless they are working directly for the persons being detained or for an independent third party working to protect human rights." The membership voted overwhelmingly in favor of the change and, in 2008, the Council voted to amend existing APA policy to make it consistent with the member-initiated referendum (for reviews of this issue, see Altman, 2008; Harris & Botticelli, 2010; Hollander, 2010; Soldz, 2008).

It took many additional years of relentless opposition by dedicated dissident psychologists, again with members of the Division of Psychoanalysis at the forefront, before APA retained outside counsel to conduct an independent investigation regarding its relationship with the military. The investigators concluded that there had been collusion between APA and members of the military in order to ensure that APA policy was kept at a high level to permit the military to engage in the enhanced interrogations of national security detainees. Once the secret collaboration between APA and military psychologists was exposed, the APA council voted 157-1 in favor of a new policy that resolved that "psychologists shall not conduct, supervise, be in the presence of, or otherwise assist any national security interrogations for any military or intelligence entities" (APA, 2015, p. 5). As a result of these efforts, as of January 2016, psychologists were removed from Guantánamo Bay.

More recently, psychoanalysts have had much to say in regard to the current refugee crises. In 2015, the American Psychoanalytic Association issued a Refugee Resettlement Position Statement, which highlights the tendency to emphasize difference and hence lose empathy for populations in need. The statement goes on to argue that we need to be sensitive not only to the trauma that refugees suffer but also to the trauma that we will cause ourselves and following generations because of complicity with the persecution of helpless people. Similarly, certain analysts have discussed the "othering" that takes place in political discourse and made the point that psychoanalysis and our understanding of the unconscious could help to combat these tendencies (Koritar, 2017; Volkan, 2017). For example, Varvin (2017) powerfully explained some of the ways that we can understand xenophobia from a psychoanalytic stance:

> Collective memories of past traumatization and humiliation may fuel various fantasies: of revenge or rectification of wrong-doing; the demand for sameness and purity being threatened by elements that endanger cohesiveness and unity; the other being cast in the role of unwanted, projected parts of the self; or, competition for scarce jobs by desperate refugees. As a defense against the perceived threat, political factions may use paranoid rhetoric stimulating fantasies against a defined enemy: the refugees. (p. 376)

Family separation is another important area in which psychoanalysis has much to offer in critique of governmental policies. The long-lasting effects of family separation and the associated trauma has been much discussed in the press and the professional literature (e.g., Santa-Maria & Cornille, 2007). The current administration has increased the practice of separating immigrant children from their families, and this has caught the attention of the psychology community. APA president Jessica Henderson Daniel, PhD, spoke out in May 2018 on the science behind this policy and the impact on children and families, noting in a statement and in *The New York Times* that

> the administration's policy of separating children from their families as they attempt to cross into the United States without documentation is not only needless and cruel, it threatens the mental and physical health of both the children and their caregivers. (Hirschfeld Davis & Nixon, 2018, para. 18)

A psychoanalytic lens helps us deepen this discussion as we bring issues of dissociation, emotional dysregulation, and attachment disturbances into the discourse.

In describing the role that psychologist/psychoanalysts play in responding to societal dilemmas, I am not making the claim that psychoanalysts are a uniquely ethical group. Indeed, psychoanalysts have a long history of being on both sides of important ethical divides in different cultures and historical areas. The point, rather, is that their role in helping to shape the public response to political situations can be seen as the contemporary rekindling of the socially progressive and politically engaged roots of psychoanalysis. There is something intrinsic to psychoanalysis's fundamental recognition of the limits of human rationality, the pervasiveness of self-deception, and the long-standing interest in broader social and cultural concerns that establishes a context for this type of active and progressive political engagement.

# 7

# Summary

The goal of this book is to provide an overview of key theoretical concepts and principles of intervention in contemporary psychoanalysis and psychoanalytic therapy. It describes a range of different mechanisms of action hypothesized by contemporary psychoanalysts to underlie the process of therapeutic change. The book also provides, as context, the historical and cultural background necessary to understand how psychoanalysis evolved and the factors shaping recent developments in contemporary theory and psychoanalytic practice. One of my objectives has been to correct misconceptions about psychoanalysis and psychoanalytic therapy that are based on caricatures of a style of psychoanalysis that is no longer dominant in the United States.

Psychoanalysis originated more than 100 years ago and has evolved dramatically over time. In North America it has evolved to adapt to current cultural values and needs. With the relational turn, it has become

http://dx.doi.org/10.1037/0000190-007
*Psychoanalysis and Psychoanalytic Therapies, Second Edition*, by J. D. Safran and J. Hunter

more flexible, less authoritarian, more practical, and more responsive to the needs of a wider range of clients. A growing body of empirical evidence supports the effectiveness of psychoanalytically oriented treatments. American psychoanalysis has also become more democratic, changing from a tradition that was dominated by White male physicians to one that includes diverse psychologists, social workers, licensed psychoanalysts, and other mental health professionals.

Nonetheless, psychoanalysis has retained the qualities that define it as a distinct and powerful treatment approach and theory of mind. It remains a form of treatment that emphasizes careful listening for unconscious material, and particularly internal conflict; an understanding of the influence of developmental experiences on current functioning; and an emphasis on the importance of the therapeutic relationship as both a source of information and a curative factor. It remains an open-ended and potentially long-term form of therapy that allows for deep engagement.

Psychoanalysis has been criticized by both the behavioral tradition and the tradition of humanistic psychology. The behavioral tradition has critiqued psychoanalysis for its lack of scientific legitimacy. The traditional antipathy of many psychoanalysts to empirical research has been a serious problem—one that has served to maintain the insularity of the tradition, forestalled critical self-reflection, and led to treating theory as if it were fact. For these reasons, the current resurgence of interest in empirical research among psychoanalysts is all to the good. Nevertheless, it would be a mistake to disregard or devalue those dimensions of psychoanalysis that fall outside of the natural sciences—those aspects of psychoanalysis that are more accurately conceptualized as a hermeneutic discipline, a critical theory, a philosophy of life, a wisdom tradition, or a craft.

The humanistic critique of psychoanalysis for its mechanistic stance, which can lead to a failure to appreciate and affirm the fundamental nobility and dignity of human nature, is also valuable. It is important to acknowledge that people have reported traumatic experiences with psychoanalytic therapy where they left treatment feeling fragmented, objectified, and pathologized rather than appreciated, understood, valued, and whole. Marvin Goldfried, one of the founders of the cognitive-behavioral tradition and a leader in the psychotherapy integration movement, conducted a research project in which he and his students used rating scheme to code transcripts of therapy sessions identified by either psychodynamic or cognitive behavior therapists as "good sessions" (Goldfried, Raue, & Castonguay, 1998). When he presented the study at conferences, he would often summarize their findings (somewhat tongue in cheek) in the following way: Whereas the cognitive therapists conveyed the message to clients that "you're better off than you think," the psychodynamic therapists tended to convey the message that "you're worse off than you think."

This summary of the findings makes sense. The emphasis in psychoanalysis has always been to help clients become aware of and acknowledge aspects of themselves that they are defended against. Traditionally the cognitive-behavioral emphasis has been on helping clients to see the way in which they selectively focus on the negative rather than the positive. The optimistic flavor of cognitive therapy and the emphasis on the positive is consistent with a long tradition of optimism and positive thinking characteristic of American culture. It can be seen in the massive success of the self-help industry and the new age emphasis on healing through positive thinking.

Optimism is an important American "natural resource." It inspired the establishment of a modern democracy and provided opportunities to immigrants who lived lives of persecution, oppression, and poverty in their homelands. It has also fueled technological innovations that were once unimaginable. At the same time, however, our American optimism can lead to an oppressive attitude that marginalizes and silences those who are suffering and judges them as failures or implicitly as morally inadequate. In a book written in the wake of her own personal struggle with breast cancer, the journalist Barbara Ehrenreich (2009) critiqued what she referred to as our "relentless promotion of positive thinking" in America and pointed out that despite this value Americans rank only 23rd in self-reported happiness relative to other nations. In this book,

Ehrenreich spoke about her tremendous sense of isolation while struggling with breast cancer because of the cultural pressure to deal with her experience in a "positive way." For example, she wrote that at one point she posted a statement on a breast cancer support group bulletin board that conveyed some of her despair and anger. In response, Ehrenreich reported receiving a "chorus of rebukes" (p. 32).

The late Stephen A. Mitchell (1993), one of the founding fathers of relational psychoanalysis, described the difference between Freud's perspective and a more contemporary American psychoanalytic perspective in the following fashion: "Freud was not a particularly cheerful fellow and his version of the rational scientific person is not an especially happy person. But this person is stronger, more grounded, more in line with reality even if it's a somber reality" (p. 305). According to Mitchell, the emphasis in contemporary psychoanalysis has shifted away from Freud's emphasis renouncing instinctual wishes and illusions toward the creation of personal meaning and the revitalization of the self. Mitchell wrote the following:

> Many patients (these days) are understood to be suffering not from conflictual infantile passions that can be tamed and transformed through reason and understanding, but from stunted personal development.... What today's psychoanalysis provides is the opportunity to freely discover and playfully explore one's own subjectivity, one's own imagination. (p. 25)

My sense is that contemporary American psychoanalysis has come to incorporate some of the more positive, creative, and affirmative qualities of the humanistic psychology of the 1960s. At the same time, I believe that it will be important for the future of psychoanalysis not to discard what many have described as Freud's tragic sensibility—his belief that there is an inherent conflict between instinct and civilization, his emphasis on the importance of acknowledging and accepting the hardships, cruelties, and indignities of life without the consolation of illusory beliefs. As indicated earlier, Freud saw the goal of psychoanalysis as one of transforming neurotic misery into ordinary human unhappiness. This can be interpreted as a modest and pessimistic perspective, but it can also be viewed as a realistic and profoundly liberating perspective—not unlike the Zen perspective that enlightenment involves letting go of the fantasy of escaping the realities of everyday life.

There is a well-known anecdote that when Freud was crossing the Atlantic with Jung and Ferenczi to deliver his lectures at Clark University, Jung spoke excitedly and enthusiastically about the growing interest in psychoanalysis by Americans. Freud was much more measured in his reaction and is reputed to have replied, "Little do they realize we are bringing the plague" (Fairfield, Layton, & Stack, 2002, p. 1). As psychoanalysis became increasingly popular in the United States, many European analysts responded ambivalently. On one hand, it is difficult to argue with success. On the other hand, they were concerned that American psychoanalysis was losing the more radical and subversive qualities that were intrinsic to the original vision of psychoanalysis. Historian Nathan Hale (1971), for example, wrote the following:

> The Americans modified psychoanalysis to solve a conflict between the radical implications of Freud's views and the pulls of American culture. . . . They muted sexuality and aggression, making both more amiable. They emphasized social conformity. They were more didactic, moralistic, and popular than Freud. They were also more optimistic and environmentalistic. (p. 332)

Psychoanalysis has a potentially powerful voice in response to current societal and political controversies and in response to the trend toward oversimplification in psychotherapy theory. Although this voice has been marginalized within the psychology community, excellent books have been published that are designed to reach out to an audience beyond the professional world. These books attempt to present a more contemporary version of American psychoanalysis that is in tune with a contemporary cultural sensibility (Gabbard, 2010; Leiper & Maltby, 2004; Lemma, 2003; Maroda, 2009; McWilliams, 1994, 2004; Renik, 2006; Summer & Barber, 2009; Wachtel, 2007, 2014). Additionally, Nancy McWilliams (2004) has done a superb job of writing about psychoanalysis in a voice that makes it accessible to a broad contemporary audience. This has been my objective as well. At the same time, however, I hope that I have managed to convey my belief that although today's psychoanalysis is very different from Freud's psychoanalysis or the orthodox American analysis of the mid-20th century, it has retained the essential elements that changed the way we think about our minds. From the very beginning, psychoanalysis had a revolutionary and subversive quality to it that challenged conventional cultural norms and values.

The marginalization of psychoanalysis has brought things full circle, back to the early days where it liberated us from conventional thinking. No longer an expression of the status quo, psychoanalysis has a renewed potential of expressing its intrinsic search for truth and becoming a constructive countercultural force. It has the opportunity to recover and build on some of its revolutionary, subversive, and culturally progressive qualities and be an important voice in psychotherapy theory as well as in the social and political challenges of our time. Psychoanalysis has changed the way we regard our minds and the human endeavor, and now its embrace of the search for truth beyond cultural limits has the potential to help change our world.

# Glossary of Key Terms

ALLIANCE (THERAPEUTIC ALLIANCE, WORKING ALLIANCE)
The client's and therapist's ability to collaborate in the therapeutic process or to negotiate a constructive collaboration.

ATTACHMENT THEORY   A developmental theory originating in the writing of John Bowlby that stipulates that human beings have a biologically wired-in propensity for maintaining proximity to attachment figures (e.g., their parents).

COMPROMISE FORMATION   A theoretical proposition emerging from the ego psychology tradition that stipulates that all experience and action is the result of a compromise between an underlying instinctually derived wish and a defense against it.

CONTAINMENT   A model of development and therapeutic change originating in the work of Wilfred Bion that stipulates that the therapist's ability to process the client's difficult or "intolerable" affective experience in a nondefensive fashion, and to help him or her make sense of it, is a central therapeutic mechanism.

COUNTERTRANSFERENCE   Historically conceptualized as the therapist's responses to the client that are influenced by the therapist's unresolved conflicts. In contemporary psychoanalytic theory, countertransference tends to be conceptualized as the totality of the therapist's experience while with the client and as an important source of information.

DEFENSE   An intrapsychic process that functions to avoid emotional pain by in one way or another pushing thoughts, wishes, feelings, or fantasies out of awareness. Common examples of defenses are intellectualization, repression, reaction formation, splitting, and projection.

DISSOCIATION   A partial or complete disruption of the normal integration of a person's conscious or psychological functioning resulting from anxiety or trauma. Involves the splitting of different self-states or self-experiences from one another.

ENACTMENT   Takes place when client and therapist unwittingly get caught in playing out a particular relational scenario that is influenced by both the client's and therapist's unique personalities, relational styles, blind spots, sensitivities, and so on. Enactments are ubiquitous in psychotherapy.

EVENLY SUSPENDED ATTENTION (EVENLY HOVERING ATTENTION)   An attentive, open, and receptive listening style in which the therapist attempts to listen to whatever the client says without allowing his or her preconceptions or expectations to shape what he or she attends to.

INSIGHT   A mechanism of change that has always been considered as important by psychoanalysts. Insight involves becoming aware of a feeling, wish, fantasy, thought, or memory that has previously been unconscious. Insight can also involve becoming aware of how one's previous experiences or current unconscious expectations or beliefs are shaping self-defeating interpersonal patterns in the present.

INTERNALIZATION   The process of developing an internal representation of relationships with others that shapes our ongoing experience and actions. There are many different theories of internalization. Internalization is considered to play an important role in the developmental process and to be an important mechanism of change in psychotherapy.

INTERNAL OBJECTS (INTERNAL OBJECT RELATIONS)   Hypothetical psychic structures developed through a combination of real interactions with others, fantasy, and defensive (self-protective) processes. These psychic structures shape our experience of others, the type of partners we tend to choose (romantic and otherwise), and the way in which we experience relationships with others. There are many different models of internal object relations, each with its own assumptions and both theoretical and practical implications.

INTERPRETATION   The therapist's attempt to help make sense of the client's experience, articulate a hypothesis about the client's unconscious experience, or draw the client's attention to unconscious self-defeating interpersonal patterns.

INTERSECTIONALITY   The interconnected nature of social factors such as race, class, and ethnicity and the associated discrimination as applied to individuals or groups.

INTRAPSYCHIC CONFLICT   A conflict between unconscious wishes and defenses against them.

MENTALIZATION   The capacity to see ourselves and others as beings with psychological depth and underlying mental states including desires, feelings, and beliefs. Mentalization is also the capacity to access and reflect on our own thoughts, feelings, and motivations and to reflect on the mental states of others.

METACOMMUNICATION   An intervention that involves engaging the client in the process of stepping back collaboratively and exploring what is implicitly taking place in the therapeutic relationship.

ONE-PERSON PSYCHOLOGY   The perspective in traditional or classical psychoanalysis that assumes it is possible to understand the client's intrapsychic processes out of context of the therapist's ongoing contributions to the interaction. From this perspective, the client's transference is viewed as a distorted perception influenced by the client's past and projected onto a neutral stimulus.

PRIMARY PROCESS   A raw or primitive form of psychic functioning that begins at birth and continues to operate unconsciously throughout the lifetime. In primary process, there is no distinction between past, present, and future. Different feelings and experiences can be condensed together into one image or symbol, feelings can be expressed metaphorically, and the identities of different people can be merged. Primary process can be seen operating in dreams and fantasy.

RESISTANCE   Conceptualized as the tendency for the client to resist change or act in a way that undermines the therapeutic process. There are multiple factors underlying resistance, such as ambivalence about changing, a fear of losing one's sense of self, and a reaction to a problematic intervention by the therapist. The exploration of resistance is viewed as a central objective in psychoanalysis.

RUPTURE (RUPTURE IN THE THERAPEUTIC ALLIANCE, RUPTURE IN THE THERAPEUTIC RELATIONSHIP, THERAPEUTIC IMPASSE)   Viewed as an inevitable occurrence in therapy that varies in intensity, duration, and frequency. The process of working through alliance ruptures or therapeutic impasses constructively is viewed as an important mechanism of change.

SECONDARY PROCESS   The style of psychic functioning associated with consciousness. It is the foundation for rational, reflective thinking. It is logical, sequential, and orderly.

TRANSFERENCE   The client's tendency to view the therapist in terms that are shaped by his or her experiences with important caregivers and other significant figures in his or her developmental process. In contemporary psychoanalytic theory, the transference is always influenced to varying degrees by the therapist's real characteristics.

TWO-PERSON PSYCHOLOGY   The perspective common to many contemporary psychoanalytic models that assumes that both therapist and client are always contributing to everything that takes place in the therapeutic relationship. From this perspective, one cannot develop a meaningful understanding of the client's intrapsychic processes and actions without developing an understanding of the way in which they are being influenced by the therapist.

UNCONSCIOUS   A central psychoanalytic construct that is conceptualized in different ways by different psychoanalytic theories. Common threads running through all of these theories are the premises that (a) our experience and actions are influenced by psychological processes that are not part of our conscious awareness and (b) these unconscious processes are kept out of awareness in order to avoid psychological pain.

# References

Abbass, A. A., Kisely, S. R., Town, J. M., Leichsenring, F., Driessen, E., De Maat, S., . . . Crowe, E. (2014). Short-term psychodynamic psychotherapies for common mental disorders. *Cochrane Database of Systematic Reviews, 2014*(7), CD004687. http://dx.doi.org/10.1002/14651858.CD004687.pub4

Abraham, K. (1949). *Selected papers of Karl Abraham.* London, England: Hogarth Press.

Ainsworth, M., Blehar, M. C., Waters, E., & Wall, S. (1978). *Patterns of attachment: A psychological study of the Strange Situation.* Hillsdale, NJ: Erlbaum.

Akhtar, S. (2006). Technical challenges faced by the immigrant psychoanalyst. *The Psychoanalytic Quarterly, 75,* 21–43. http://dx.doi.org/10.1002/j.2167-4086.2006.tb00031.x

Alexander, F. (1948). *Fundamentals of psychoanalysis.* New York, NY: Norton.

Altman, N. (2000). Black and white thinking: A psychoanalyst reconsiders race. *Psychoanalytic Dialogues, 10,* 589–605. http://dx.doi.org/10.1080/10481881009348569

Altman, N. (2008). The psychodynamics of torture. Coercive interrogations and the mental health profession. *Psychoanalytic Dialogues, 18,* 658–670. http://dx.doi.org/10.1080/10481880802297681

Altman, N. (2010). *The analyst in the inner city: Race, class, and culture through a psychoanalytic lens.* New York, NY: Routledge.

American Psychiatric Association. (1980). *Diagnostic and statistical manual of mental disorders* (3rd ed.). Washington, DC: Author.

American Psychoanalytic Association. (2015). *Refugee resettlement position statement.* Retrieved from http://www.apsa.org/sites/default/files/Final%20 Draft%20-%20Position%20Statement%20on%20Refugee%20Resettlement.pdf

American Psychological Association. (2015). *Resolution to amend the 2006 and 2013 Council Resolutions to clarify the roles of psychologists related to interrogation and detainee welfare in national security settings, to further implement the 2008 Petition Resolution, and to safeguard against acts of torture and cruel, inhuman, or degrading treatment or punishment in all settings.* Retrieved from http://www.apa.org/independent-review/psychologists-interrogation.pdf

American Psychological Association. (2017). *Ethical principles of psychologists and code of conduct* (2002, Amended June 1, 2010, and January 1, 2017). Retrieved from http://www.apa.org/ethics/code/index.aspx

American Psychological Association. (2017). *Multicultural guidelines: An ecological approach to context, identity, and intersectionality.* Retrieved from http://www.apa.org/about/policy/multicultural-guidelines.pdf

Arlow, J., & Brenner, C. (1964). *Psychoanalytic concepts and the structural theory.* Oxford, England: International Universities Press.

Aron, L. (1996). *A meeting of minds: Mutuality in psychoanalysis.* Hillsdale, NJ: The Analytic Press.

Aron, L. (1999). Clinical choices and the relational matrix. *Psychoanalytic Dialogues, 9,* 1–29. http://dx.doi.org/10.1080/10481889909539301

Aron, L. (2006). Analytic impasse and the third: Clinical implications of intersubjectivity theory. *The International Journal of Psycho-Analysis, 87,* 349–368. http://dx.doi.org/10.1516/15EL-284Y-7Y26-DHRK

Aron, L., & Starr, K. E. (2012). *A psychotherapy for the people.* New York, NY: Routledge.

Bader, M. J. (1994). The tendency to neglect therapeutic aims in psychoanalysis. *The Psychoanalytic Quarterly, 63,* 246–270. http://dx.doi.org/10.1080/21674086.1994.11927414

Barber, J. P., Muran, J. C., McCarthy, K. S., & Keefe, R. J. (2013). Research on psychodynamic therapies. In M. J. Lambert (Ed.), *Bergin and Garfield's handbook of psychotherapy and behavior change* (6th ed., pp. 443–494). New York, NY: Wiley & Sons.

Barber, J. P., Muran, J. C., McCarthy, K. S., & Keefe, R. J. (in press). Research on psychodynamic therapies. In M. Barham, W. Lutz, & L. Castonguy (Eds.), *Bergin and Garfield's handbook of psychotherapy and behavior change* (7th ed.). New York, NY: Wiley & Sons.

Bateman, A., & Fonagy, P. (2008). 8-year follow-up of patients treated for borderline personality disorder: Mentalization-based treatment versus treatment as usual. *The American Journal of Psychiatry, 165,* 631–638. http://dx.doi.org/10.1176/appi.ajp.2007.07040636

Bateman, A., & Fonagy, P. (2016). *Mentalization-based treatment for personality disorders.* Oxford, England: Oxford University Press. http://dx.doi.org/10.1093/med:psych/9780199680375.001.0001

Beebe, B., & Lachmann, F. M. (2002). *Infant research and adult treatment.* Hillsdale, NJ: The Analytic Press.

Benjamin, J. (1988). *The bonds of love.* New York, NY: Pantheon Books.

Benjamin, J. (1990). An outline of intersubjectivity: The development of recognition. *Psychoanalytic Psychology, 7,* 33–46. http://dx.doi.org/10.1037/h0085258

Benjamin, J. (1995). Sameness and difference: Toward an "overinclusive" model of gender development. *Psychoanalytic Inquiry, 15,* 125–142. http://dx.doi.org/10.1080/07351699509534021

Benjamin, J. (2004). Beyond doer and done to: An intersubjective view of thirdness. *The Psychoanalytic Quarterly, 73,* 5–46. http://dx.doi.org/10.1002/j.2167-4086.2004.tb00151.x

Benjamin, J. (2018). *Beyond doer and done to: Recognition theory, intersubjectivity and the third.* New York, NY: Routledge.

Bergin, A. E., & Strupp, H. S. (1973). *Changing frontiers in the science of psychotherapy.* Chicago, IL: Aldine.

Binder, J. (2004). *Key competencies in brief dynamic psychotherapy.* New York, NY: Guilford Press.

Bion, W. R. (1970). *Attention and interpretation.* London, England: Routledge.

Bollas, C. (1992). *Being a character: Psychoanalysis and self experience.* New York, NY: Routledge.

Bordin, E. (1979). The generalizability of the psychoanalytic concept of the working alliance. *Psychotherapy: Theory, Research, & Practice, 16,* 252–260. http://dx.doi.org/10.1037/h0085885

Botticelli, S. (2004). The politics of relational psychoanalysis. *Psychoanalytic Dialogues, 14,* 635–651. http://dx.doi.org/10.1080/10481880409353130

Bowlby, J. (1969). *Attachment and loss: Vol. 1. Attachment.* New York, NY: Basic Books.

Bowlby, J. (1973). *Attachment and loss: Vol. 2. Separation, anxiety and anger.* New York, NY: Basic Books.

Bowlby, J. (1980). *Attachment and loss: Vol. 3. Sadness and depression.* New York, NY: Basic Books.

Bresler, J., & Starr, K. (Eds.). (2015). *Relational psychoanalysis and psychotherapy integration: An evolving synergy.* New York, NY: Routledge. http://dx.doi.org/10.4324/9781315747422

Breuer, J., & Freud, S. (1955). Studies on hysteria. In J. Strachey (Ed. & Trans.), *The standard edition of the complete psychological works of Sigmund Freud*

(Vol. 2, pp. 1–305). London, England: Hogarth Press. (Original work published 1893–1895)

Bromberg, P. M. (1995). Resistance, object-usage, and human relatedness. *Contemporary Psychoanalysis, 31*, 173–191. http://dx.doi.org/10.1080/00107530.1995.10746903

Bromberg, P. M. (1998). *Standing in the spaces: Essays on clinical process, trauma, and dissociation*. Hillsdale, NJ: The Analytic Press.

Bromberg, P. M. (2006). *Awakening the dreamer: Clinical journeys*. Hillsdale, NJ: The Analytic Press.

Cassidy, J., & Shaver, P. R. (Eds.). (2016). *Handbook of attachment: Theory, research, and clinical applications*. New York, NY: Guilford Press.

Chambless, D. L., & Hollon, S. D. (1998). Defining empirically supported therapies. *Journal of Consulting and Clinical Psychology, 66*, 7–18. http://dx.doi.org/10.1037/0022-006X.66.1.7

Clarkin, J. F., Levy, K. N., Lenzenweger, M. F., & Kernberg, O. F. (2007). Evaluating three treatments for borderline personality disorder: A multiwave study. *The American Journal of Psychiatry, 164*, 922–928. http://dx.doi.org/10.1176/ajp.2007.164.6.922

Coltart, N. (2000). *Slouching towards Bethlehem*. New York, NY: Guilford Press.

Connors, M. (2006). *Symptom-focused dynamic psychotherapy*. Hillsdale, NJ: The Analytic Press.

Cooper, S. (2000). *Objects of hope: Exploring possibility and limit in psychoanalysis*. Hillsdale, NJ: The Analytic Press.

Crenshaw, K. (2020). *On intersectionality: Essential writings*. New York, NY: New Press.

Cushman, P. (1995). *Constructing the self, constructing America*. Reading, MA: Addison-Wesley.

Cushman, P., & Gilford, P. (2000). Will managed care change our way of being? *American Psychologist, 55*, 985–996. http://dx.doi.org/10.1037/0003-066X.55.9.985

Danto, E. (2005). *Freud's free clinics*. New York, NY: Columbia University Press. http://dx.doi.org/10.7312/dant13180

Davanloo, H. (Ed.). (1980). *Short-term dynamic psychotherapy*. New York, NY: Aronson.

Davies, J. M. (1996). Linking the "pre-analytic" with the post-classical: Integration, dissociation, and the multiplicity of unconscious process. *Contemporary Psychoanalysis, 32*, 553–576. http://dx.doi.org/10.1080/00107530.1996.10746336

Davies, J. M. (2004). Whose bad object are we anyway? Repetition and our elusive love affair with evil. *Psychoanalytic Dialogues, 14*, 711–732. http://dx.doi.org/10.1080/10481881409348802

Dimen, M. (2003). *Sexuality, intimacy, power*. Hillsdale, NJ: The Analytic Press.

Dimen, M. (2010). Reflections on cure, or "I/Thou/It." *Psychoanalytic Dialogues, 20,* 254–268. http://dx.doi.org/10.1080/10481885.2010.481612

Drescher, J. (2008). A history of homosexuality and organized psychoanalysis. *Journal of the American Academy of Psychoanalysis and Dynamic Psychiatry, 36,* 443–460. http://dx.doi.org/10.1521/jaap.2008.36.3.443

Dreyfus, H. E., & Dreyfus, S. L. (1986). *Mind over machine*. New York, NY: Free Press.

Driessen, E., Hegelmaier, L. M., Abbass, A. A., Barber, J. P., Dekker, J. J. M., Van, H. L., . . . Cuijpers, P. (2015). The efficacy of short-term psychodynamic psychotherapy for depression: A meta-analysis update. *Clinical Psychology Review, 42,* 1–15. http://dx.doi.org/10.1016/j.cpr.2015.07.004

Eagle, M. (1984). *Recent developments in psychoanalysis*. New York, NY: McGraw-Hill.

Ehrenberg, D. (1992). *The intimate edge*. New York, NY: Norton.

Ehrenreich, B. (2009). *Bright-sided: How the relentless promotion of positive thinking has undermined America*. New York, NY: Macmillan.

Ekman, P. (1993). Facial expression and emotion. *American Psychologist, 48,* 384–392. http://dx.doi.org/10.1037/0003-066X.48.4.384

Ekman, P., & Davidson, R. J. (Eds.). (1994). *The nature of emotions: Fundamental questions*. New York, NY: Oxford University Press.

Etchegoyen, H. (1991). *The fundamentals of psychoanalytic technique*. London, England: Karnac Books.

Eubanks, C. F., Muran, J. C., & Safran, J. D. (2018). Alliance rupture repair: A meta-analysis. *Psychotherapy: Theory, Research, & Practice, 55,* 508–519. http://dx.doi.org/10.1037/pst0000185

Fairbairn, W. R. D. (1952). *Psychoanalytic studies of the personality*. London, England: Routledge and Kegan Paul.

Fairbairn, W. R. D. (1994). *Psychoanalytic studies of the personality*. New York, NY: Routledge/Taylor & Francis.

Fairfield, S., Layton, L., & Stack, C. (Eds.). (2002). *Bringing the plague: Toward a postmodern psychoanalysis*. New York, NY: Other Press.

Fenichel, O. (1945). *Problems of psychoanalytic technique*. New York, NY: Psychoanalytic Quarterly.

Ferenczi, S. (1980a). *Final contributions to the problems and methods of psychoanalysis* (M. Balint, Ed. and E. Mosbacher, Trans.). London, England: Karnac Books.

Ferenczi, S. (1980b). *Further contributions to the problems and methods of psychoanalysis* (J. Richman, Ed. and J. Suttie, Trans.). London, England: Karnac Books.

Ferenczi, S., & Rank, O. (1956). *The development of psychoanalysis.* New York, NY: Dover. (Original work published 1925)

Ferro, A. (2002). *In the analyst's consulting room.* New York, NY: Routledge.

Fonagy, P., Gergely, G., Jurist, E., & Target, M. (2002). *Affect regulation, mentalization, and the development of self.* New York, NY: Other Press.

Fonagy, P., Kachle, H., Krause, R., Jones, E., Perron, R., & Lopez, L. (1999). *An open door review of outcome studies in psychoanalysis.* London, England: University College.

Fonagy, P., Steele, H., & Steele, M. (1991). Maternal representations of attachment during pregnancy predict the organization of infant–mother attachment at one year of age. *Child Development, 62,* 891–905. http://dx.doi.org/10.2307/1131141

Fosha, D. (2000). *The transforming power of affect: A model for accelerated change.* New York, NY: Basic Books.

Frank, K. A. (1999). *Psychoanalytic participation, action, interaction, and integration.* Hillsdale, NJ: The Analytic Press.

Freud, A. (1936). *The ego and the mechanisms of defense.* Honolulu, HI: Hogarth Press.

Freud, S. (1912). The dynamics of transference. In *The standard edition of the complete psychological works of Sigmund Freud* (Vol. 12). London, England: Hogarth Press.

Freud, S. (1920). *A general introduction to psychoanalysis* (G. S. Hall, Trans., p. 247). New York, NY: Boni and Liveright.

Freud, S. (1953). The interpretation of dreams. In *The standard edition of the complete psychological works of Sigmund Freud* (Vols. 4–5; J. Strachey, Trans. & Ed.). London, England: Hogarth Press. (Original work published 1900)

Freud, S. (1955). Studies on hysteria. In *The standard edition of the complete psychological works of Sigmund Freud* (Vol. 2; J. Breuer & S. Freud, Eds.). London, England: Hogarth Press. (Original work published 1895)

Freud, S. (1958). Recommendations to physicians practising psychoanalysis. In *The standard edition of the complete psychological works of Sigmund Freud* (Vol. 12, p. 115). London, England: Hogarth Press and the Institute of Psychoanalysis. (Original work published 1912)

Freud, S. (1961). The ego and the id. In *The standard edition of the complete psychological works of Sigmund Freud* (Vol. 19, pp. 3–66; J. Strachey, Trans. & Ed.). London, England: Hogarth Press. (Original work published 1923)

Freud, S. (1965). New introductory lectures on psychoanalysis. In *The standard edition of the complete psychological works of Sigmund Freud* (Vol. 22, p. 100; J. Strachey, Trans. & Ed.). London, England: Norton. (Original work published 1933)

Frew, J., & Spiegler, M. (2012). *Contemporary psychotherapies for a diverse world* (1st rev. ed.). New York, NY: Routledge.

Frijda, N. H. (1986). *The emotions*. New York, NY: Cambridge University Press.

Fromm, E. (1941). *A man for himself.* New York, NY: Rinehart.

Gabbard, G. O. (2010). *Long-term psychodynamic psychotherapy*. Arlington, VA: American Psychiatric Publishing.

Galatzer-Levy, R., Bachrach, H., Skolnikoff, A., & Waldron, S. (2000). *Does psychoanalysis work?* New Haven, CT: Yale University Press.

Gay, P. (1988). *Freud: A life for our time.* New York, NY: Norton.

Gentile, K. (2013). Bearing the cultural in order to engage in a process of witnessing. *Psychoanalytic Psychology, 30,* 456–470. http://dx.doi.org/10.1037/a0032056

Ghent, E. (1990). Masochism, submission, surrender: Masochism as a perversion of surrender. *Contemporary Psychoanalysis, 26,* 108–136. http://dx.doi.org/10.1080/00107530.1990.10746643

Gold, J., & Stricker, G. (2015). Assimilative psychodynamic psychotherapy: An active, integrative psychoanalytic approach. In J. Bressler & K. Starr (Eds.), *Relational psychoanalysis and psychotherapy integration: An evolving synergy* (pp. 39–56). New York, NY: Routledge.

Goldfried, M. R., Raue, P. J., & Castonguay, L. G. (1998). The therapeutic focus in significant sessions of master therapists: A comparison of cognitive-behavioral and psychodynamic-interpersonal interventions. *Journal of Consulting and Clinical Psychology, 66,* 803–810. http://dx.doi.org/10.1037/0022-006X.66.5.803

Goldfried, M. R., & Wolfe, B. E. (1996). Psychotherapy practice and research. Repairing a strained alliance. *American Psychologist, 51,* 1007–1016. http://dx.doi.org/10.1037/0003-066X.51.10.1007

Greenberg, J. (1986). Theoretical models and the analyst's neutrality. *Contemporary Psychoanalysis, 22,* 87–106. http://dx.doi.org/10.1080/00107530.1986.10746117

Greenberg, J., & Mitchell, S. A. (1983). *Object relations in psychoanalytic theory.* Cambridge, MA: Harvard University Press. http://dx.doi.org/10.2307/j.ctvjk2xv6

Greenberg, J., & Safran, J. (1987). *Emotions in psychotherapy: Affect, cognition, and process of change.* New York, NY: Guilford Press.

Greenson, R. R. (1965). The working alliance and the transference neurosis. *The Psychoanalytic Quarterly, 34,* 155–181. http://dx.doi.org/10.1080/21674086.1965.11926343

Grunbaum, F. (1984). *The foundations of psychoanalysis: A philosophical critique.* Berkeley: University of California Press.

Guignon, C. (2004). *On being authentic*. London, England: Routledge. http://dx.doi.org/10.4324/9780203646793

Gutwill, S., & Hollander, N. C. (2006). Class and splitting in the clinical setting: The ideological dance in the transference and countertransference. In L. Layton, N. C. Hollander, & S. Gutwill (Eds.), *Psychoanalysis, class, and politics: Encounters in the clinical setting* (pp. 92–106). New York, NY: Routledge.

Hale, N. (1971). *Freud and the Americans: The beginnings of psychoanalysis in the United States, 1876–1917* (Vol. 1). Oxford, England: Oxford University Press.

Hale, N. (1995). *The rise and crisis of psychoanalysis in the United States: Freud and the Americans 1917–1985* (Vol. 2). Oxford, England: Oxford University Press.

Haley, J. (1997). *Leaving home: The therapy of disturbed young people*. New York, NY: Routledge.

Harris, A. (2008). *Gender as soft assembly*. Hillsdale, NJ: The Analytic Press.

Harris, A., & Botticelli, S. (2010). *First do no harm: The paradoxical encounters of psychoanalysis, warmaking, and resistance*. New York, NY: Routledge.

Hartmann, H. (1964). *Ego psychology and the problem of adaptation*. New York, NY: International Universities Press.

Hirschfeld Davis, J., & Nixon, R. (2018, May 29). Trump officials, moving to break up migrant families, blame Democrats. *The New York Times*. Retrieved from https://www.nytimes.com/2018/05/29/us/politics/trump-democrats-immigrant-families.html

Hoffman, I. Z. (1998). *Ritual and spontaneity in the psychoanalytic process: A dialectical-constructivist view*. Hillsdale, NJ: The Analytic Press.

Hoffman, I. Z. (2009). Doublethinking our way to "scientific" legitimacy: The desiccation of human experience. *Journal of the American Psychoanalytic Association, 57*, 1043–1069. http://dx.doi.org/10.1177/0003065109343925

Hollander, N. C. (1997). *Love in a time of hate*. New Brunswick, NJ: Rutgers University Press.

Hollander, N. C. (2006). Psychoanalysis and the problem of the bystander in times of terror. In L. Layton, N. C. Hollander, & S. Gutwill (Eds.), *Psychoanalysis, class, and politics: Encounters in the clinical setting* (pp. 154–165). New York, NY: Routledge.

Hollander, N. C. (2010). *Uprooted minds: Surviving the politics of terror in the Americas*. New York, NY: Routledge.

Holmes, J. (2010). *Exploring in security: Towards an attachment-informed psychoanalytic psychotherapy*. New York, NY: Routledge.

Horowitz, A. V. (2003). *The making of mental illness*. Chicago, IL: Chicago University Press.

Howard, K. I., Kopta, S. M., Krause, M. S., & Orlinsky, D. E. (1986). The dose-effect relationship in psychotherapy. *American Psychologist, 41,* 159–164. http://dx.doi.org/10.1037/0003-066X.41.2.159

Huber, D., Henrich, G., Gastner, J., & Klug, G. (2012). Must all have prizes? The Munich Psychotherapy Study. In R. Levy, J. S. Ablon, & H. Kaechele (Eds.), *Evidence-based psychodynamic psychotherapy II* (pp. 51–69). Totowa, NJ: Humana Press. http://dx.doi.org/10.1007/978-1-60761-792-1_4

Jacobs, T. (1991). *The use of the self: Countertransference and communication in the analytic setting.* Madison, CT: International Universities Press.

Jacoby, R. (1983). *The repression of psychoanalysis: Otto Fenichel and the political Freudians.* Hillsdale, NJ: The Analytic Press.

Joseph, B. (1989). *Psychic equilibrium and psychic change.* London, England: Tavistock and Routledge.

Keefe, J. R., McCarthy, K. S., Dinger, U., Zilcha-Mano, S., & Barber, J. P. (2014). A meta-analytic review of psychodynamic therapies for anxiety disorders. *Clinical Psychology Review, 34,* 309–323. http://dx.doi.org/10.1016/j.cpr.2014.03.004

Kivlighan, D. M., III, Goldberg, S. B., Abbas, M., Pace, B. T., Yulish, N. E., Thomas, J. G., . . . Wampold, B. E. (2015). The enduring effects of psychodynamic treatments vis-à-vis alternative treatments: A multilevel longitudinal meta-analysis. *Clinical Psychology Review, 40,* 1–14. http://dx.doi.org/10.1016/j.cpr.2015.05.003

Klein, M. (2002a). *The writings of Melanie Klein: Vol. 1. Love, guilt, and reparation and other works, 1921–1945.* New York, NY: Free Press. (Original work published 1955)

Klein, M. (2002b). *The writings of Melanie Klein: Vol. 3. Envy and gratitude and other works, 1946–1963.* New York, NY: Free Press. (Original work published 1975)

Knight, R. P. (1953). The present status of organized psychoanalysis in the United States. *Journal of the American Psychoanalytic Association, 1,* 197–221. http://dx.doi.org/10.1177/000306515300100201

Kohut, H. (1984). *How does analysis cure?* Chicago, IL. University of Chicago Press.

Koritar, E. (2017). Shining a psychoanalytic light on alienation, otherness, and xenophobia. *American Journal of Psychoanalysis, 77,* 341–346. http://dx.doi.org/10.1057/s11231-017-9114-5

Lacan, J. (1988a). *The seminar of Jacques Lacan: Book 1. Freud's papers on technique, 1953–1954* (J. Miller & J. Forrester, Trans. & Ed.). New York, NY: Norton. (Original work published 1975)

Lacan, J. (1988b). *The seminar of Jacques Lacan: Book 2. The ego in Freud's theory and in the technique of psychoanalysis 1954–1955* (J. Miller & S. Tomaselli, Trans. & Ed.). New York, NY: Norton. (Original work published 1978)

Leary, K. (2000). Racial enactments in dynamic treatment. *Psychoanalytic Dialogues, 10,* 639–653. http://dx.doi.org/10.1080/10481881009348573

Leichsenring, F., Biskup, J., Kreische, R., & Staats, H. (2005). The Göttingen study of psychoanalytic therapy: First results. *The International Journal of Psycho-Analysis, 86,* 433–455. http://dx.doi.org/10.1516/XX6F-AU0W-KWM3-G6LU

Leichsenring, F., Klein, S., & Salzer, S. (2014). The efficacy of psychodynamic psychotherapy in specific mental disorders: A 2013 update of empirical evidence. *Contemporary Psychoanalysis, 50*(1–2), 89–130. http://dx.doi.org/10.1080/00107530.2014.880310

Leichsenring, F., Leweke, F., Klein, S., & Steinert, C. (2015). The empirical status of psychodynamic psychotherapy—an update: Bambi's alive and kicking. *Psychotherapy and Psychosomatics, 84*(3), 129–148. http://dx.doi.org/10.1159/000376584

Leichsenring, F., Luyten, P., Hilsenroth, M. J., Abbass, A., Barber, J. P., Keefe, J. R., . . . Steinert, C. (2015). Psychodynamic therapy meets evidence-based medicine: A systematic review using updated criteria. *The Lancet Psychiatry, 2,* 648–660. http://dx.doi.org/10.1016/S2215-0366(15)00155-8

Leiper, R., & Maltby, M. (2004). *The psychodynamic approach to therapeutic change.* London, England: Sage.

Lemma, A. (2003). *Introduction to the practice of psychoanalytic psychotherapy.* Chichester, England: Wiley & Sons. http://dx.doi.org/10.1002/9780470713426

Levenson, H. (2017). *Brief dynamic therapy* (2nd ed.). Washington, DC: American Psychological Association. http://dx.doi.org/10.1037/0000043-000

Levy, R., Ablon, J. S., & Kaechele, H. (Eds.). (2012). *Evidence-based psychodynamic psychotherapy* (2nd ed.). New York, NY: Humana Press. http://dx.doi.org/10.1007/978-1-60761-792-1

Lewis, N. A. (2004, November 30). *Red Cross finds detainee abuse in Guantánamo.* Retrieved from https://www.nytimes.com/2004/11/30/politics/red-cross-finds-detainee-abuse-in-guantanamo.html

Lichtenberg, J. (1989). *Psychoanalysis and motivation.* Hillsdale, NJ: The Analytic Press.

Loewald, H. W. (1960). On the therapeutic action of psycho-analysis. *The International Journal of Psycho-Analysis, 41,* 16–33.

Luborsky, L. (1984). *Principles of psychoanalytic psychotherapy: A manual for supportive-expressive treatment.* New York, NY: Basic Books.

Luborsky, L., Diguer, L., Seligman, D. A., Rosenthal, R., Krause, E. D., Johnson, S., . . . Schweizer, E. (1999). The researcher's own therapy allegiances: A "wild card" in comparisons of treatment efficacy. *Clinical Psychology: Science and Practice, 6,* 95–106. http://dx.doi.org/10.1093/clipsy/6.1.95

Lyons-Ruth, K., Bruschweiler-Stern, N., Harrison, A. M., Morgan, A. C., Nahum, J. P., Sander, L., . . . Tronick, E. Z. (1998). Implicit relational knowing: Its role in development and psychoanalytic treatment. *Infant Mental Health Journal*, *19*, 282–289. http://dx.doi.org/10.1002/(SICI)1097-0355(199823)19:3<282: AID-IMHJ3>3.0.CO;2-O

Main, M., Kaplan, N., & Cassidy, J. (1985). Security in infancy, childhood, and adulthood: A move to the level of representation. *Monographs of the Society for Research in Child Development*, *50*, 66–104. http://dx.doi.org/ 10.2307/3333827

Makari, G. (2008). *Revolution in mind: The creation of psychoanalysis*. New York, NY: Harper Collins.

Makari, G. (2015). *Soul machine: The invention of the modern mind*. New York, NY: Norton.

Malan, D. H. (1963). *A study of brief psychotherapy*. New York, NY: Plenum Press.

Maroda, K. (2009). *Psychodynamic techniques: Working with emotion in the therapeutic relationship*. New York, NY: Guilford Press.

McCullough Valliant, L. M. (1997). *Changing character: Short-term anxiety regulating psychotherapy for restructuring defenses, affects, and attachment*. New York, NY: Basic Books.

McMain, S. F., Links, P. S., Gnam, W. H., Guimond, T., Cardish, R. J., Korman, L., & Streiner, D. L. (2009). A randomized trial of dialectical behavior therapy versus general psychiatric management for borderline personality disorder. *The American Journal of Psychiatry*, *166*, 1365–1374. http://dx.doi.org/10.1176/ appi.ajp. 2009.09010039

McWilliams, N. (1994). *Psychoanalytic diagnosis: Understanding personality structure in the clinical process*. New York, NY: Guilford Press.

McWilliams, N. (2004). *Psychoanalytic psychotherapy: A practitioner's guide*. New York, NY: Guilford Press.

Messer, S. B. (2015). How I have changed over time as a psychotherapist. *Journal of Clinical Psychology*, *71*, 1104–1114. http://dx.doi.org/10.1002/jclp.22220

Messer, S. B., & Warren, C. S. (1995). *Models of brief psychotherapy*. New York, NY: Guilford Press.

Mitchell, S. A. (1988). *Relational concepts in psychoanalysis*. Cambridge, MA: Harvard University Press.

Mitchell, S. A. (1993). *Hope and dread in psychoanalysis*. New York, NY: Basic Books.

Mitchell, S. A. (1997). *Influence and autonomy in psychoanalysis*. Hillsdale, NJ: The Analytic Press.

Moncayo, R. (2008). *Evolving Lacanian perspectives for clinical psychoanalysis*. London, England: Karnac Books.

Moskowitz, M. (1996). The social consequence of psychoanalysis. In R. M. Perez Foster & R. A. Javier (Eds.), *Reaching across boundaries of culture and class: Widening the scope of psychotherapy* (pp. 21–46). Northvale, NJ: Aronson.

Muran, J. C., Safran, J. D., Gorman, B. S., Samstag, L. W., Eubanks-Carter, C., & Winston, A. (2009). The relationship of early alliance ruptures and their resolution to process and outcome in three time-limited psychotherapies for personality disorders. *Psychotherapy: Theory, Research, & Practice, 46,* 233–248. http://dx.doi.org/10.1037/a0016085

Norcross, J. C., & Goldfried, M. R. (2019). *Handbook of psychotherapy integration* (3rd ed.). Oxford, England: Oxford University Press.

Norcross, J. C., & Lambert, M. J. (2018). Psychotherapy relationships that work III. *Psychotherapy: Theory, Research, & Practice, 55,* 303–315. http://dx.doi.org/10.1037/pst0000193

Ogden, T. (1994). *Subject of analysis.* Northvale, NJ: Aronson.

Padrón, C. (2019). The political potentiality of the psychoanalytic process. In P. Gherovici & C. Christian (Eds.), *Psychoanalysis in the barrios: Race, class and the unconscious* (pp. 189–202). New York, NY: Routledge.

Parkinson, B. (1995). *Ideas and realities of emotion.* London, England: Routledge.

Parsons, M. (2000). *The dove that returns, the dove that vanishes: Paradox and creativity in psychoanalysis.* London, England: Routledge.

Perez Foster, R. M., Moskowitz, M., & Javier, R. A. (Eds.). (1996). *Reaching across boundaries of culture and class: Widening the scope of psychotherapy.* Northvale, NJ: Aronson.

Persons, J. B., & Silberschatz, G. (1998). Are results of randomized controlled trials useful to psychotherapists? *Journal of Consulting and Clinical Psychology, 66,* 126–135. http://dx.doi.org/10.1037/0022-006X.66.1.126

Pizer, S. A. (1998). *Building bridges: The negotiation paradox in psychoanalysis.* Hillsdale, NJ: The Analytic Press.

Plotkin, M. B. (2001). *Freud in the Pampas: The emergence and development of psychoanalytic culture in Argentina.* Stanford, CA: Stanford University Press.

Pogue White, K. (2002). Surviving hate and being hated: Some thoughts about racism from a psychoanalytic perspective. *Contemporary Psychoanalysis, 38,* 401–422. http://dx.doi.org/10.1080/00107530.2002.10747173

Rank, O. (1929). *The trauma of birth.* New York, NY: Harcourt, Brace.

Rayner, E. (1991). *The independent mind in British psychoanalysis.* Northvale, NJ: Aronson.

Reich, W. (1941). *Character analysis.* New York, NY: Orgone Institute Press.

Reiff, P. (1966). *The triumph of the therapeutic: Uses of faith after Freud.* Chicago, IL: University of Chicago Press.

Reik, T. (1948). *Listening with the third ear: The inner experience of a psychoanalyst.* New York, NY: Farrar, Straus, & Giroux.

Renik, O. (1993). Analytic interaction: Conceptualizing technique in light of the analyst's irreducible subjectivity. *The Psychoanalytic Quarterly, 62,* 553–571. http://dx.doi.org/10.1080/21674086.1993.11927393

Renik, O. (2006). *Practical psychoanalysis for therapists and patients.* New York, NY: Other Press.

Rice, L. N., & Greenberg, L. S. (1984). *Patterns of change: Intensive analysis of psychotherapy process.* New York, NY: Guilford Press.

Richardson, P., Kachele, H., & Renlund, C. (2004). *Research on psychoanalytic psychotherapy with adults.* New York, NY: Karnac Books.

Ringstrom, P. A. (2007). Scenes that write themselves: Improvisational moments in relational psychoanalysis. *Psychoanalytic Dialogues, 17,* 69–99. http://dx.doi.org/10.1080/10481880701301303

Safran, J. D. (1984). Assessing the cognitive-interpersonal cycle. *Cognitive Therapy and Research, 8,* 333–347. http://dx.doi.org/10.1007/BF01173309

Safran, J. D. (1993). Breaches in the therapeutic alliance: An arena for negotiating authentic relatedness. *Psychotherapy: Theory, Research, & Practice, 30,* 11–24. http://dx.doi.org/10.1037/0033-3204.30.1.11

Safran, J. D. (1998). *Widening the scope of cognitive therapy: The therapeutic relationship, emotion, and the process of change.* Northvale, NJ: Aronson.

Safran, J. D. (1999). Faith, despair, will, and the paradox of acceptance. *Contemporary Psychoanalysis, 35,* 5–23. http://dx.doi.org/10.1080/00107530.1999.10746378

Safran, J. D. (2001). When worlds collide: Psychoanalysis and the empirically supported treatment movement. *Psychoanalytic Dialogues, 11,* 659–681. http://dx.doi.org/10.1080/10481881109348635

Safran, J. D. (2002). Brief relational psychoanalytic treatment. *Psychoanalytic Dialogues, 12,* 171–195. http://dx.doi.org/10.1080/10481881209348661

Safran, J. D. (2003). The relational turn, the therapeutic alliance and psycho-therapy research: Strange bedfellows or postmodern marriage? *Contemporary Psychoanalysis, 39,* 449–475. http://dx.doi.org/10.1080/00107530.2003.10747215

Safran, J. D. (2016). Agency, surrender, and grace in psychoanalysis. *Psychoanalytic Psychology, 33,* 58–72. http://dx.doi.org/10.1037/a0038020

Safran, J. D. (2017). The unbearable lightness of being: Authenticity and the search for the real. *Psychoanalytic Psychology, 34,* 69–77. http://dx.doi.org/10.1037/pap0000093

Safran, J. D., Crocker, P., McMain, S., & Murray, P. (1990). Therapeutic alliance rupture as a therapy event for empirical investigation. *Psychotherapy: Theory, Research, & Practice, 27,* 154–165. http://dx.doi.org/10.1037/0033-3204.27.2.154

Safran, J. D., & Greenberg, L. S. (1991). *Emotion, psychotherapy, and change.* New York, NY: Guilford Press.

Safran, J. D., Greenberg, L. S., & Rice, L. N. (1988). Integrating psychotherapy research and practice: Modeling the change process. *Psychotherapy: Theory, Research, & Practice, 25,* 1–17. http://dx.doi.org/10.1037/h0085305

Safran, J. D., & Kraus, J. (2015). Relational techniques in a cognitive-behavioral therapy context: "It's bigger than the both of us." In N. C. Thoma & D. McKay (Eds.), *Working with emotion in cognitive-behavioral therapy: Techniques for clinical practice* (pp. 333–355). New York, NY: Guilford Press.

Safran, J. D., & Muran, J. C. (1994). Toward a working alliance between research and practice. In P. F. Talley, H. H. Strupp, & J. F. Butler (Eds.), *Psychotherapy research and practice* (pp. 206–226). New York, NY: Basic Books.

Safran, J. D., & Muran, J. C. (1996). The resolution of ruptures in the therapeutic alliance. *Journal of Consulting and Clinical Psychology, 64,* 447–458. http://dx.doi.org/10.1037/0022-006X.64.3.447

Safran, J. D., & Muran, J. C. (Eds.). (1998). *The therapeutic alliance in brief psychotherapy.* Washington, DC: American Psychological Association. http://dx.doi.org/10.1037/10306-000

Safran, J. D., & Muran, J. C. (2000). *Negotiating the therapeutic alliance: A relational treatment guide.* New York, NY: Guilford Press.

Safran, J. D., & Muran, J. C. (2006). Has the concept of the therapeutic alliance outlived its usefulness? *Psychotherapy: Theory, Research, & Practice, 43,* 286–291. http://dx.doi.org/10.1037/0033-3204.43.3.286

Safran, J. D., Muran, J. C., Samstag, L. W., & Stevens, C. (2001). Repairing alliance ruptures. *Psychotherapy: Theory, Research, & Practice, 38,* 406–412. http://dx.doi.org/10.1037/0033-3204.38.4.406

Safran, J. D., Muran, J. C., Samstag, L. W., & Stevens, C. (2002). Repairing alliance ruptures. In J. C. Norcross (Ed.), *Psychotherapy relationships that work* (pp. 235–254). New York, NY: Oxford University Press.

Safran, J. D., & Segal, Z. V. (1990). *Interpersonal process in cognitive therapy.* New York, NY: Basic Books.

Saketopoulou, A. (2011). Minding the gap: Intersections between gender, race, and class in work with gender variant children. *Psychoanalytic Dialogues, 21,* 192–209. http://dx.doi.org/10.1080/10481885.2011.562845

Saks, E. (2008). *The center cannot hold: My journey through madness.* New York, NY: Hyperion Press.

Sandell, R., Blomberg, J., Lazar, A., Carlsson, J., Broberg, J., & Schubert, J. (2000). Varieties of long-term outcome among patients in psychoanalysis and long-term psychotherapy. A review of findings in the Stockholm Outcome of Psychoanalysis and Psychotherapy Project (STOPP). *The International Journal of Psycho-Analysis, 81,* 921–942. http://dx.doi.org/10.1516/0020757001600291

Santa-Maria, M. L., & Cornille, T. (2007). Traumatic stress, family separations, and attachment among Latin American immigrants. *Traumatology, 13*(2), 26–31. http://dx.doi.org/10.1177/1534765607302278

Sayers, J. (2001). *Kleinians: Psychoanalysis inside out.* Oxford, England: Blackwell.

Schafer, R. (1968). *Aspects of internalization.* Madison, CT: International Universities Press.

Schön, D. (1983). *The reflective practitioner.* New York, NY: Basic Books.

Seligman, M. E. P. (1995). The effectiveness of psychotherapy. The Consumer Reports study. *American Psychologist, 50,* 965–974. http://dx.doi.org/10.1037/0003-066X.50.12.965

Shedler, J. (2010). The efficacy of psychodynamic psychotherapy. *American Psychologist, 65,* 98–109. http://dx.doi.org/10.1037/a0018378

Sifneos, P. E. (1972). *Short-term psychotherapy and emotional crisis.* Cambridge, MA: Harvard University Press.

Slavin, M. O., & Kriegman, D. (1998). Why the analyst needs to change: Toward a theory of conflict, negotiation, and mutual influence in the therapeutic process. *Psychoanalytic Dialogues, 8,* 247–284. http://dx.doi.org/10.1080/10481889809539246

Soldz, S. (2008). Healers or interrogators: Psychology and the United States torture regime. *Psychoanalytic Dialogues, 18,* 592–613. http://dx.doi.org/10.1080/10481880802297624

Steele, M., & Steele, H. (2008). *Clinical applications of the Adult Attachment Interview.* New York, NY: Guilford Press.

Steele, M., & Steele, H. (2018). *Handbook of attachment-based interventions.* New York, NY: Guilford Press.

Sterba, R. (1934). The fate of the ego in analytic therapy. *The International Journal of Psycho-Analysis, 15,* 117–126.

Stern, D. B. (1997). *Unformulated experience.* Hillsdale, NJ: The Analytic Press.

Stern, D. B. (2010). *Partners in thought: Working with unformulated experience, dissociation, and enactment.* New York, NY: Routledge. http://dx.doi.org/10.4324/9780203880388

Stern, D. N. (1985). *The interpersonal world of the infant: A view from psychoanalysis and developmental psychology.* New York, NY: Basic Books.

Stern, D. N., Sander, L. W., Nahum, J. P., Harrison, A. M., Lyons-Ruth, K., Morgan, A. C., . . . the Process of Change Study Group. (1998). Non-interpretive mechanisms in psychoanalytic therapy. The 'something more' than interpretation. *The International Journal of Psycho-Analysis, 79,* 903–921.

Sternberg, R., & Jordan, J. (Eds.). (2005). *A handbook of wisdom: Psychological perspectives.* New York, NY: Cambridge University Press. http://dx.doi.org/10.1017/CBO9780511610486

Stiles, W., & Shapiro, D. (1989). Abuse of the drug metaphor in psychotherapy process-outcome research. *Clinical Psychology Review, 9,* 521–543. http://dx.doi.org/10.1016/0272-7358(89)90007-X

Strachey, J. (1934). The nature of the therapeutic action of psychoanalysis. *The International Journal of Psycho-Analysis, 15,* 127–159.

Strupp, H. H., & Binder, J. L. (1984). *Psychotherapy in a new key: A guide to time limited dynamic psychotherapy.* New York, NY: Basic Books.

Sullivan, H. S. (1953). *The interpersonal theory of psychiatry.* New York, NY: Norton.

Summer, R. F., & Barber, J. P. (2009). *Psychodynamic therapy: A guide to evidence based practice.* New York, NY: Guilford Press.

Talley, F., Strupp, H., & Butler, S. (1994). *Psychotherapy research and practice: Bridging the gap.* New York, NY: Basic Books.

Taylor, C. (1992). *The ethics of authenticity.* Cambridge, MA: Harvard University Press.

Thompson, C. (1957). *Psychoanalysis: Evolution and development.* New York, NY: Atlantic Monthly Press.

Thompson, M. G. (2004). *The ethic of honesty: The fundamental rule of psycho-analysis.* New York, NY: Rodopi.

Tronick, E. (2007). *The neurobehavioral and social-emotional development of infants and children.* New York, NY: Norton.

Tummala-Narra, P. (2016). *Psychoanalytic theory and cultural competence in psychotherapy* [Kindle edition]. Washington, DC: American Psychological Association. http://dx.doi.org/10.1037/14800-000

VandenBos, G. (2015). *APA dictionary of psychology* (2nd ed.). Washington, DC: American Psychological Association.

Varvin, S. (2017). Our relations to refugees: Between compassion and dehumanization. *American Journal of Psychoanalysis, 77,* 359–377. http://dx.doi.org/10.1057/s11231-017-9119-0

Volkan, V. (2017). *Immigrants and refugees: Trauma, perennial mourning, prejudice and border psychology.* London, England: Karnac.

Wachtel, P. L. (1977). *Psychoanalysis and behavior therapy: Toward an integration.* New York, NY: Basic Books.

Wachtel, P. L. (1997). *Psychoanalysis, behavior therapy, and the relational world.* Washington, DC: American Psychological Association. http://dx.doi.org/10.1037/10383-000

Wachtel, P. L. (2007). *Relational theory and the practice of psychotherapy.* New York, NY: Guilford Press.

Wachtel, P. L. (2011). *Therapeutic communication: Knowing what to say when.* New York, NY: Guilford Press.

Wachtel, P. L. (2014). *Cyclical psychodynamics: The inner world, the intimate world, and the world of culture and society.* New York, NY: Routledge. http://dx.doi.org/10.4324/9781315794037

Wampold, B. (2001). *The great psychotherapy debate: Models, methods, findings.* Northvale, NJ: Erlbaum.

Westen, D. (1998). Unconscious thought, feeling, and motivation: The end of a century long debate. In R. Bornstein & J. Masling (Eds.), *Empirical perspectives on the psychoanalytic unconscious. Empirical studies of psychoanalytic theories* (pp. 1–43). Washington, DC: American Psychological Association. http://dx.doi.org/10.1037/10256-001

Westen, D., & Gabbard, G. (1999). Psychoanalytic approaches to personality. In L. Pervin & O. John (Eds.), *Handbook of personality: Theory and research* (pp. 57–101). New York, NY: Guilford Press.

Westen, D., Novotny, C. M., & Thompson-Brenner, H. (2004). The empirical status of empirically supported psychotherapies: Assumptions, findings, and reporting in controlled clinical trials. *Psychological Bulletin, 130,* 631–663. http://dx.doi.org/10.1037/0033-2909.130.4.631

Winnicott, D. W. (1958). *Through paediatrics to psycho-analysis: Collected papers.* New York, NY: Basic Books.

Winnicott, D. W. (1965). *The maturational process and the facilitating environment.* New York, NY: International Universities Press.

Yi, K. (2014). Toward formulation of ethnic identity beyond the binary of white oppressor and racial other. *Psychoanalytic Psychology, 31,* 426–434. http://dx.doi.org/10.1037/a0036649

Young-Bruehl, E. (2006). Coming of age in New York City: Two homeless boys. *The Psychoanalytic Quarterly, 75,* 323–343. http://dx.doi.org/10.1002/j.2167-4086.2006.tb00042.x

# Index

# About the Authors

**Jeremy D. Safran, PhD,** was a professor of psychology and former director of clinical training at the New School for Social Research in New York City. He was also senior research scientist at Beth Israel Medical Center. He was a faculty member at the New York University postdoctoral program in psychotherapy and psychoanalysis and a member at the Stephen A. Mitchell Center for Relational Studies. He was also past president of the International Association for Relational Psychoanalysis and Psychotherapy. He was a founding board member of the Sandor Ferenczi Center.

Dr. Safran was an associate editor for the journal *Psychoanalytic Dialogues* and was on the editorial boards of *Psychotherapy Research* and *Psychoanalytic Psychology*. He published more than 100 articles and chapters and several books, including *Negotiating the Therapeutic Alliance: A Relational Treatment Guide*, *Emotion in Psychotherapy*, *The Therapeutic Alliance in Brief Psychotherapy*, *Interpersonal Process in Cognitive Therapy*, and *Psychoanalysis and Buddhism: An Unfolding Dialogue*.

Dr. Safran and his colleagues conducted research on the topic of therapeutic impasses for more than 2 decades. He was also known for his work on emotion in psychotherapy and for his integration of principles from Buddhist psychology into psychoanalysis and psychotherapy.

**Jennifer Hunter, PhD,** is an adjunct professor in the counseling program and a clinical supervisor at Brooklyn College. She has a private practice in New York City. She is also a clinical associate at the New School for Social Research and is on the board of the Sandor Ferenczi Center. She is a graduate of the New York University Clinical Psychology doctoral program and received an Advanced Certification in Couples and Family Therapy from the New York University Postdoctoral Program in Psychotherapy and Psychoanalysis.

# About the Series Editor

**Matt Englar-Carlson, PhD,** is a professor of counseling and director of the Center for Boys and Men at California State University–Fullerton. A Fellow of the American Psychological Association (APA), Dr. Englar-Carlson's scholarship focuses on training helping professionals to work more effectively with boys and men across the full range of human diversity. His publications and presentations are focused on men and masculinities, social justice and diversity issues in psychological training and practice, and theories of psychotherapy. Dr. Englar-Carlson coedited the books *In the Room With Men: A Casebook of Therapeutic Change, Counseling Troubled Boys: A Guidebook for Professionals, Beyond the 50-Minute Hour: Therapists Involved in Meaningful Social Action*, and *A Counselor's Guide to Working With Men*, and he was featured in the APA-produced video *Engaging Men in Psychotherapy*. He was named Researcher of the Year, Professional of the Year, and he received the Professional Service award from the Society for the Psychological Study of Men and Masculinities, and was one of the core authors of the *APA Guidelines for Professional Psychological Practice With Boys and Men*. As a clinician, Dr. Englar-Carlson has worked with children, adults, and families in school, community, and university mental health settings. He is the coauthor of *Adlerian Psychotherapy*, which is part of the Theories of Psychotherapy Series.